Corporate Interiors

No. 7

Corporate Interiors

No. 7

Roger Yee

Visual Reference Publications Inc., New York

Left: Fulbright & Jaworski L.L.P., Los Angeles, California **Design firm:** DMJM Rottet **Photography:** Nick Merrick Hedrich Blessing.

Corporate Interiors No. 7

PUBLISHER	Larry Fuersich larry@visualreference.com
ASSOCIATE PUBLISHER	Bill Ash bill@visualreference.com
EDITORIAL DIRECTOR	Roger Yee yeerh@aol.com
CREATIVE ART DIRECTOR	Veronika Cherepanina veronika@visualreference.com
MARKETING MANAGER	Marc Cohen marc@visualreference.com
PRODUCTION MANAGER	John Hogan johnhvrp@yahoo.com
CIRCULATION MANAGER	Amy Yip amy@visualreference.com
CONTROLLER	Angie Goulimis angie@visualreference.com

www.visualreference.com

Visual Reference Publications, Inc.
302 Fifth Avenue
New York, NY 10001
Tel: 212.279.7000 • Fax: 212.279.7014

Distributors to the trade in the United States and Canada
Watson-Guptill
770 Broadway
New York, NY 10003

Distributors outside the United States and Canada
HarperCollins International
10 East 53rd Street
New York, NY 10022-5299

Library of Congress Cataloging in Publication Data:
Corporate Interiors No. 7

Printed in China

The book is exclusively distributed in China
by Beijing Designerbooks Co., Ltd.
Building No.2, No.3, Babukou, Gulouxidajie,
Xicheng District, Beijing 100009, P.R.China
Tel: 0086(010)6406-7653 Fax: 0086(010)6406-0931
E-mail: info@designerbooks.net
http://www.designerbooks.net

ISBN: 1-58471-092-6

Book Design: Veronika Cherepanina

thinkglobal

Value is always in style.

4C GLOBAL years

CAPRICE SEATING.   1.800.220.1900 USA   1.877.446.2251 CAN   WWW.GLOBALTOTALOFFICE.COM

IIDEX Awards
NeoCon Canada

THE SAMUEL HALL – CURRELLY GALLERY, ONE OF TORONTO'S GREAT INTERIORS, WAS BUILT DURING THE 1930'S TO THE HIGHEST ARCHITECTURAL STANDARDS. RECENTLY TRANSFORMED, THIS MAGNIFICENT HALL ADDS A NEW LEVEL OF STYLE AND COMFORT FOR THE VISITOR TO THE MUSEUM, PRESENTING A WARM ENVIRONMENT IN WHICH TO REST, REFLECT, GATHER AND SOCIALIZE.

nienkämper AT THE ROYAL ONTARIO MUSEUM

You will also find Nienkämper Furniture lounges inside all of the new galleries offering attractive views of the architecture and collections.

Nienkämper Furniture – *is one of the most respected names in the North American Design Industry.*

HBF. P.O. Box 8, Hickory NC 28603. For information, call 1.800.423.9614 or www.hbf.com

H B F

Contents

Introduction

Desperate Cube Farmers

*T*his can't be real. How can a young office worker accomplish anything while functioning like a communications Tower of Babel? He or she can often be seen simultaneously conducting a conversation on a Motorola Razr cell phone, listening to music on a portable Apple iPod MP3 player connected to Boze Companion speakers and surfing the Internet on an HP Media Center PC. Yet the work gets done.

Is this the kind of employee the corporate world expects to assign to one of Dilbert's "cube farms" or other conventional office accommodations? The odds aren't good. Employers are discovering that the typical Generation Y individual straddles boundaries of every kind, a development that is already sending ripples through the office environment.

However, business leaders needn't be so alarmed if they consider the revolution in workflow, work style and career path they set in motion in the late 20th century. Take workflow. Tasks that once occurred under one roof are increasingly distributed across time zones, continents and companies. For example, major components for the new Boeing 787 Dreamliner will be designed and fabricated in locations as far flung as Japan and France by companies like Mitsubishi and Messier-Dowty before Boeing assembles them in the United States.

Work style is no longer uniform for all employees in the office, with growing numbers taking work to cafeterias, satellite offices, home offices and the road. Not only do many public and private places offer wireless Internet connection, laptop computers can be equipped for cellular Internet service where there's no Starbucks in sight. And talk about career path with anyone under age 30. If companies feel any obligation towards today's workers, it's to give them meaningful work and a chance to acquire new skills. Young employees expect nothing more.

New office environments designed by the nation's leading architects and interior designers take these changes into account, because the organizations they serve realize the new ways of working bring opportunities as well as challenges. Even a casual glance at the impressive new offices featured in Corporate Interiors No. 7 will show readers a corporate world that's moving away from the cubicle farms and rabbit warrens of the recent past. Come along for a visit, and don't be surprised if you find imaginative new environments where your colleagues might feel like rolling up their sleeves and multi-tasking.

Roger Yee
Editor

INSCAPE

inscapesolutions.com

Archideas/Lee Stout, Inc.

Archideas
311 West Superior Street
Chicago, IL 60610
312.951.1106
312.951.0442 (Fax)
www.archideas.com

Lee Stout, Inc.
348 West 36th Street
New York, NY 10018
212.594.4563
212.268.5579 (Fax)
www.leestoutinc.com

Archideas/Lee Stout, Inc.

Morningstar
Chicago, Illinois

Convinced that comprehensive information about mutual fund performance should be widely available to individual investors, a Chicago securities analyst named Joe Mansueto created a company in his one-bedroom apartment in 1984 that has become one of the most admired brands in the financial world. Today, Morningstar is a trusted source of information on stocks, mutual funds, variable annuities, closed-end funds, exchange-traded funds, separate accounts, hedge funds and 529 college savings funds. Yet it remains a spirited, informal, people-focused business that continues to reflect the founder and chairman's love of design, ability to adapt new technologies and philosophy of growing a business by investing in it. One of the latest examples of the Morningstar approach to business is the innovative, new, 20,000-square-foot office floor, designed by Archideas/Lee Stout, Inc., that was recently added to its corporate headquarters

Above: Landmark informal meeting area.

Opposite top: Café.

Opposite bottom: Team space & Landmark in open office space.

Photography: Christopher Barrett/Hedrich Blessing.

11

Archideas/Lee Stout, Inc.

in Chicago. This space, which houses a computer facility, national sales group, and administrative functions including accounting, human resources, corporate systems, corporate communications and design, meets goals that provide an intriguing portrait of the company. Morningstar's design brief calls for a space for self-described "scrappy upstarts," a space that exemplifies core values of honesty and creativity, a space featuring a variety of work settings that empower employees to change personal work spaces, a loose spatial definition of the functional groups within the space, and multiple spaces for employee collaboration, communication and concentration. The design does a remarkably good job of transforming this design brief into a dynamic open work environment with a genuine sense of place. To satisfy "scrappy upstarts," for example, such rough, industrial building materials as tectum, particle board,

Below: Casual meeting space.
Bottom: Home base with landmarks.
Left: Formal meeting space.

13

Archideas/Lee Stout, Inc.

carpet tile, and perforated steel, and such exposed infrastructure as HVAC ducts, electrical conduit and sprinklers dramatically contrast with refined yet light-hearted furnishings. Architectural forms are modeled in unconventional and quixotic ways, and color and pattern assume provocative and playful roles. Furthermore, honesty and creativity are nurtured with an open workspace that reveals work in progress, whiteboards that make work visible and invite comment, a café, communication centers and other spaces that encourage chance meetings, and spaces for collaboration and contemplation that are integrated into the workspace. Employees are empowered through flexible project spaces where teamwork is facilitated, easy-to-modify furniture such as rolling tables, freestanding storage, adjustable chairs and task lighting, and open-plan work stations in which everyone is accessible, including the CEO. Landmark structures that serve as points of reference, different planning methods that are used to define work neighborhoods, and shared spaces that buffer adjacent neighborhoods introduce a loose yet workable spatial definition of functional groups so the open space has shape and direction. And changes in lighting,

Right: Tea point.
Top: Technical home base.

Archideas/Lee Stout, Inc.

Left: Home base with integrated lounge seating.

Bottom left: Elevator lobby.

Bottom right: Touch down space.

enclosures, whiteboards and common spaces are among the numerous cues distributed throughout the floor to identify spaces dedicated to collaboration, communication and concentration. There's ample reason to presume that the design is succeeding for Morningstar, which has refrained from instituting major changes to the space. After all, it wouldn't take long for one of the financial world's most trusted sources of information to uncover a convincing reason for change.

Aref & Associates

100 N. Sepulveda Blvd.
Suite 100
El Segundo, CA 90245
310.414.1000
310.414.1099 (Fax)
www.aref.com

Aref & Associates

The Boston Consulting Group
Los Angeles, California

It's only natural for an international strategy and management-consulting firm, whose mission is to help leading corporations create and sustain competitive advantage, to turn a critical eye on itself in developing its own workplace. Consequently, when the Los Angeles office of The Boston Consulting Group asked Aref & Associates to design its new, 25,000 square-foot office in the Wells Fargo Center, a prestigious downtown skyscraper, it requested a highly functional yet warm and inviting environment for its 100 employees. The facility features shared private offices for consultants collaborative team spaces and "commons" for group activity, and open work stations for administrative personnel, reflecting the firm's spatial requirements. Its open structure is decidedly pragmatic and efficient, with private offices and team spaces enclosed within mostly glass partitions that simultaneously confer acoustical privacy and transmit daylight and views to interior areas. Such appointments as movingue wood, low-iron glass, carpeting, stylish ergonomic office furniture, a water feature and a stunning art collection also acknowledge the importance of a collegial atmosphere for one of the world's leading management consulting firms. The firm has grown from a single office in Boston, opened by founder Bruce D. Henderson in 1963, to 53 offices in the Americas, Europe and Asia/Pacific today.

Above: Private offices.
Right: Reception desk.
Bottom right: Lounge area.
Opposite bottom left: Lobby.
Opposite bottom right: Conference room.
Photography: Paul Bielenberg.

The Boston Consulting C

Aref & Associates

NWQ Investment Management Company, LLC
Los Angeles, California

Below: Reception/lobby.

Opposite top: Conference room.

Opposite bottom right: Corridor.

Opposite bottom left: Trading room.

Photography: Paul Bielenberg.

How does an emerging and tightly knit organization retain its sense of community and collaboration after expanding from one floor in an office building to two and a half floors? This was the recent scenario confronted by Los Angeles-based NWQ Investment Management Company, LLC, a subsidiary of Nuveen Investments, Inc. founded in 1982. The investment management firm takes pride in sustaining an environment for its value-oriented investment teams that fosters their independence in terms of corporate culture, management style and investment philosophies. To preserve this spirit following the expansion, Aref & Associates has designed the 66,000 square-foot facility to link all three floors with an interconnecting stair and introduce a common area on each level for mingling and collaboration. Thus, against a backdrop of private offices for analysts, open trading work stations for traders, and open work stations for administrative and operational personnel, the design showcases a three-story interior stair with a dramatic water feature, ergonomic furnishings, a warm color scheme, direct and indirect lighting, and such complementary materials as lacewood, anigre and cherry woods, marble, granite, cast glass, ornamental metal and an impressive art collection to integrate the workplace. The 200 employees of NWQ may be divided by design, but they're united by it as well.

Aref & Associates

New Urban West, Inc.
Santa Monica, California

Building homes in Southern California for over 50 years has given New Urban West a valuable perspective on moving people into new environments. For this reason, its own recent relocation of 45 employees from a closed, private office setting to a more collaborative, open-plan workplace, designed by Aref & Associates, has been carefully orchestrated to be smooth and trouble-free. Although the new 10,745 square-foot space occupies a former industrial facility,

a cold, high-tech look was not considered desirable for such accommodations as the reception area, private offices, open-plan work stations, conference rooms, staff lounge, galley and computer room. For this reason, the open industrial ceiling that preserves the building's full floor-to-slab height is countered by vintage original glass pendants and up lighting along the perimeter and core walls, such materials as African mahogany and ebony woods, upholstered walls,

carpet, stained MDF panels, steel posts and an impressive art collection, and comfortable, contemporary furnishings. This major homebuilder, now focused on high-end residential communities, has come home to a warm and inviting place of its own.

Above: Conference room.
Right: Conference room.
Opposite bottom left: Workstations.
Opposite bottom right: Open office area.
Photography: Paul Bielenberg.

Aref & Associates

Comcast Corporation
Los Angeles, California

Above: Corridor.
Left: Café.
Below left: Reception.
Bottom left: Conference room.
Photography: Paul Bielenberg.

With 21.4 million cable customers, 8.5 million high-speed Internet customers and 1.3 million voice customers, Comcast is the nation's leading provider of cable, entertainment and communications products and services through such properties as G4, E! Entertainment Television, Style Network, The Golf Channel, Outdoor Life Network, AZN Television, PBS KIDS Sprout, TV One and four Comcast SportsNets. Size is no obstacle to its activities, now ranging from the development, management and operation of broadband cable networks and the delivery of programming content to majority ownership of two professional sports teams, which continue to expand with such ventures as Internet-based telephone service. Comcast's new 38,000 square-foot Los Angeles office, designed for 172 employees by Aref & Associates, illustrates the environment needed to support the complex nature of company activity. Its relatively open setting of private offices, conference rooms, open work stations and a commons area are tailored to support an informal, creative and intensely interactive community of workers. Given the highly technological nature of Comcast's operations, Aref & Associates has wisely finished the space with such appropriate industrial-style touches as stained concrete, European ash, ergonomic furniture, sophisticated lighting and exposed ceiling. If anything, the attractive, dynamic and accessible look of the facility seems to come naturally.

Ballinger

833 Chestnut Street
Suite 1400
Philadelphia, PA 19107
215.446.0900
215.446.0901 (Fax)
www.ballinger-ae.com
contact@ballinger-ae.com

Ballinger

Merck & Co., Inc.
North Wales, Pennsylvania

Life has been good in North Wales, a suburb of Philadelphia with some 3,320 residents, for Merck & Co. In fact, a recently completed facility of 500,000 square feet in North Wales for the global pharmaceutical company will eventually expand to a full build-out of 1.2 million square feet. As it is, the new construction already provides all the common program spaces necessary to accommodate the projected campus. Ballinger, serving as master planner and architect for Merck, designed the ensemble of buildings on the concept of linking office modules to a formal circulation concourse, with the common spaces anchoring a circulation spine at the head of the complex. Major spaces along the concourse, including the lobby, auditorium, cafeteria and fitness center, foster an active environment for the work force

Top left: Boardroom.
Top right: Main lobby.
Above: Lobby stair.
Opposite: Circulation.
Photography: Jeff Goldberg.

Ballinger

Merck & Co., Inc.
North Wales, Pennsylvania

that should serve it well as it expands. As a result, the office areas on campus can be perceived as extensions of both the circulation concourse and the surrounding formal landscape. This distinctive sense of place, combining the flexibility of use and ease of expansion that characterize the master plan, promises an effective and satisfying environment for Merck employees, representing the best of the 115-year-old company's values and culture, as the campus develops.

Top left: Café.
Top right: Auditorium pre-function space.
Left: Auditorium.
Opposite: Stair detail.

Ballinger

A Leading Management Consulting Company
Philadelphia, Pennsylvania

When a leading management consulting company selected the recently opened Cira Centre as the site of its new, 28,000-square-foot Philadelphia office, designed by Ballinger, it wasn't strictly because of the dramatic views from its windows. Cira Centre's prominent Center City location, along with its ability to accommodate the team "neighborhoods" that Ballinger created to promote team interaction among the firm's principals and associates, were more decisive factors. Yet there's no doubt the views have made a difference. Even as the primary public areas of the lobby and conferencing suites deliberately frame dramatic views of the Philadelphia Museum of Art and the Schuylkill River, glass private office fronts provide the necessary isolation for their occupants without denying natural light and glimpses of Center City to employees in the interior spaces. For all the glass used, there is warmth and comfort as well, thanks to the presence of a calm neutral color scheme, classic modern furnishings and sophisticated artificial lighting that discreetly supplements nature's own.

Top left: View from main conference room.

Top right: Circulation.

Opposite top: Main conference room.

Opposite bottom right: Pantry.

Opposite bottom left: Lobby reception.

Photography: Chun Y Lai.

Ballinger

Novo Nordisk LLC
North Brunswick, New Jersey

You won't find the open-plan enclosures that characterize corporate America in the new and largely open work environment, designed by Ballinger, of Novo Nordisk LLC in North Brunswick, New Jersey. Cubicles have no place in the corporate drive to nurture collegial interaction and innovation that has produced the 22,000-square-foot office for 50 employees of the U.S. affiliate of Novo Nordisk A/S. A Copenhagen-based world leader in diabetes care and other pharmaceutical products since 1925, Novo Nordisk A/S decided to open its first research facility in the United States in 2004, and asked Ballinger to create an environment representative of its European culture to attract a world-class research community. Appreciating the importance of natural light to European office workers, whose proximity to perimeter windows is often mandated by law, the design team developed a workplace focused on a central skylighted gathering space to draw the research community together, and grouped team spaces, conference rooms and offices around it. The dynamic, minimally detailed contemporary setting, where glass is used extensively for acoustical privacy and visual transparency, is performing just as Novo Nordisk hoped, giving it a strategic outpost in America that emulates its European counterparts.

Top left: Office space.
Above: Commons.
Left: Conference room.
Photography: Jeffrey Totaro.

BR Design Associates, LLC

411 Fifth Avenue
New York, NY 10016
212.993.9000
212.993.9001 (Fax)
www.bergerrait.com

BR Design Associates, LLC

McCann Erickson Detroit
Birmingham, Michigan

Sometimes one of the best ways to get a fresh perspective on life is to move. That's certainly one of the benefits of McCann Erickson Detroit's recent relocation from Troy, the second largest city in Michigan, with 80,959 residents (2000 Census) and the headquarters of numerous automotive and financial companies, to Birmingham, an affluent suburb of Detroit with a population of 19,291 (2000 Census) that has attracted wealthy Detroit families since its incorporation in 1864. The 350-person advertising agency, part of McCann-Erickson Worldwide, a leading global advertising agency network with offices in over 130 countries, now serves such long-term clients as General Motors, Buick and Delphi from a three-story, 90,000-square-foot office, designed by BR Design Associates, in a former

Above: Reception area.
Upper right: Exterior.
Lower right: Lobby/oculus.
Opposite: Lobby.

BR Design Associates, LLC

department store. In the new private offices, open-plan work stations, conference rooms, reception area, café and support facilities, McCann Erickson has created a lively, high density, open-plan environment. Most of the facility's private offices and conference rooms are clustered in core areas of the building's deep floors to suffuse much of the space with daylight and views and encourage internal communication as well. A central vertical circulation well, incorporating both existing escalators and a new, bleacher-style stairway meant to double as a meeting area between floors, also rein-forces the sense of openness. Appointed in drywall, maple millwork, carpet, terrazzo tile, indirect lighting and classic modern furnishings, the former department store is now dressed to sell ideas as its merchandise, allowing the venerable advertising agency, founded in 1902, to work more effectively with its most important Motor City client, currently facing one of the greatest challenges in its 109-year history.

Left: Lobby.
Far left: Conference room.
Bottom: Café.
Opposite top: Private office.

BR Design Associates, LLC

Tai Ping Carpets
New York, New York

Tai Ping is not currently a household name in the United States. However, over the course of 50 years, this Hong Kong-based custom carpet and rug company has been active in more than 100 countries, building a reputation for products that are highly suitable for luxurious and prestigious interiors, ranging from hotels and residences to yachts and private jets. To focus its efforts on establishing a higher profile in the lucrative U.S. market, the company recently opened a new, flagship showroom in New York, designed by BR Design Associates, as associate architect and project manager, and Baird Design, as design architect.

Top left: View east in showroom.
Left: Office detail.
Far left: Office corridor.
Opposite: View west in showroom.
Photography: Eric Laignel.

BR Design Associates, LLC

The one-floor, 12,000-square-foot facility, arranged in a front office-back office configuration comprising private offices, open-plan work stations, a design studio and a tea room in addition to a showroom, establishes a modern sensibility that also reflects its historic roots in Chinese culture. Inside the elegant, white interior, shaped by cast-iron columns, exposed brick vaulted ceilings, glass and drywall partitions and wood strip floors, the rich colors, textures and patterns of Tai Ping's rugs and yarns resonate like works of art. Not coincidentally, that's how Tai Ping hopes architects, interior designers and consumers see its carpets and rugs.

Top left: Detail of view east in showroom.

Top far left: Executive office.

Left: Conference room with yarn wall.

BraytonHughes Design Studios

639 Howard Street
San Francisco, CA 94105-3926
415.291.8100
415.434.8145 (Fax)
www.bhdstudios.com
info@bhdstudios.com

BraytonHughes Design Studios

Pillsbury Winthrop Shaw Pittman
Palo Alto, California

Top right: Work station.
Left: Conference room.
Bottom left: Partner's office.
Opposite: Reception/lobby atrium.
Photography: John Sutton.

While its roots date back to 1868, Pillsbury Winthrop Shaw Pittman is very much a 21st-century law firm whose 900 attorneys are leaders in capital markets, energy and technology. Its new, 2-floor, 82,000-square-foot Palo Alto office, designed by BraytonHughes Design Studios, has opened in a new, two-building complex as fast and economically as a Silicon Valley start-up. The configuration of the space, comprising an entry lobby, attorneys' and paralegals' offices, secretarial work stations, conference center, café and support areas, maximizes the number of window offices for attorneys. Even so, the understated yet sophisticated design pays attention to other critical components, such as the open area for secretarial work stations. As the attorneys observe, this long, narrow space, featuring lowered ceiling planes with pendant lighting fixtures, storage, printers and files recessed into the interior wall, blue glass transaction counters and a natural wood palette, is as critical as other workplaces at Pillsbury.

BraytonHughes Design Studios

Elevation Partners
Menlo Park, California

A client's vision of a transparent office with minimal privacy has inspired a new, one-floor, 6,000-square-foot facility for Elevation Partners in Menlo Park, designed by BraytonHughes Design Studios. Consequently, the 22 employees of Elevation Partners, a new private equity firm that will invest nearly $1.9 billion in market-leading media, entertainment, and consumer-related businesses, now occupy a distinctive environment where daylight penetrates from the perimeter walls, lined by private offices, far into the interior's open areas. Layers of glass establish the openness, beginning with full-height glazed walls for private offices, and concluding with open-plan work stations likewise fitted with glazed frames. Yet the reception area, conference rooms, private offices and media room are also distinguished by timeless materials such as Eucalyptus veneer, Jerusalem limestone, textiles and carpet, as well as comfortable modern furnishings. This deceptively simple scheme has succeeded so well that BraytonHughes is now expanding the office by 3,000 square feet.

Above: Conference room.
Top right: Partners' office.
Right: Work station.
Opposite: Reception/lobby.
Photography: John Sutton.

BraytonHughes Design Studios

Mohr Davidow Ventures
Menlo Park, California

Right: Private offices and work stations.

Bottom right: Corner detail of conference room.

Opposite: Central public space.

Photography: John Sutton.

Space may be precious along Menlo Park's legendary Sand Hill Road, where venture capitalists nurture the dreams of Silicon Valley entrepreneurs, but that shouldn't deny daylight to anyone working there. That was the position taken by Mohr Davidow Ventures in developing its new, one-floor, 12,000-square-foot office, designed by BraytonHughes Design Studios in a fresh, contemporary style using cherry and Douglas fir, carpet and limestone. The design accomplishes this feat by lining corridors of private window offices with glazing systems that "borrow" daylight for the central core of open work stations, and lifting the ceiling plane of the main gallery to match the building's sloping roofline and punching skylights into the roof. In effect, all 30 employees of Mohr Davidow, an early-stage venture capital firm investing in entrepreneurs with proven expertise in technology and science, have "window offices," along with conference rooms and a lunch room, right in Silicon Valley's epicenter.

BraytonHughes Design Studios

Morgenthaler Ventures
Menlo Park, California

Sometimes the little things make the big difference, as can be seen at the new, one-story, 12,000-square-foot Menlo Park headquarters of Morgenthaler Ventures, designed by BraytonHughes Design Studios. The workplace for 24 employees of this premier venture capital and buyout firm follows standard practice, comprising a reception-greeting area, private window offices, open-plan work stations, teleconference and meeting rooms, kitchen-dining area and mail-copy center. But the environment's graceful elegance is the product of telling details, such as patterned glass sidelights for all private offices, office doors featuring floating Eucalyptus valances that provide a sense of entry, work stations custom designed in the same Eucalyptus wood with floating laminated glass transaction counters, storage cabinets and files integrated into gypsum board enclosures, and windows affording garden views. These details and others add up to quiet luxury that suits a power-house in venture capital that has worked with over 250 entrepreneurs since its founding in 1968.

Top: Open work stations.
Right: Private office.
Photography: John Sutton.

Carrier Johnson

1301 3rd Avenue
San Diego, CA 92101
619.239.2353
619.239.6227 (Fax)
www.carrierjohnson.com

Carrier Johnson

Morrison & Foerster
San Diego, California

You notice the distinctive atmosphere immediately. The new, four-floor, 73,662-square-foot San Diego office of Morrison & Foerster, designed by Carrier Johnson, immerses visitors in a sophisticated, light-filled and appealing expression of its occupants' identity. Here is a law firm founded in 1883, currently employing some 1,020 attorneys in 19 offices worldwide, that is also one of San Diego's fastest growing law firms, with over 70 attorneys and support staff serving a diverse group of client companies. What unifies the workplace is its client focus, shaping everything from common areas, including reception, board room, training rooms and cafeteria on the first floor, to private offices, administrative workstations and conference rooms on upper floors and a law library on half of the fourth floor. Public spaces use transparent and translucent glass, matte stainless steel and such natural materials as limestone and warm woods to welcome clients to an open, gallery-like setting. There's comfort and utility too, thanks to neutral colors, informal contemporary furnishings, a water feature, quality lighting and advanced, plug/play technology that is concealed but always available. Equally important, staff members enjoy a collegial environment featuring office suites designed for interaction and a cafeteria where natural materials, outdoor views, informal seating and a surf board—saluting the southern California lifestyle—accompany meals and informal "board" meetings.

Top left: Conference room.

Top right: Board room.

Far left: Café.

Left: Elevator lobby.

Opposite: Main entry.

Photography: Scott McDonald/ Hedrich Blessing.

Carrier Johnson

RW Johnson Pharmaceutical Research Institute
La Jolla, California

Biologists and chemists may not always have reasons to converse, but the odds favor them at an outstanding new, two-story, 122,000-square-foot research facility designed by Carrier Johnson for the R.W. Johnson Pharmaceutical Research Institute in La Jolla, California. Home to the Scripps Institution of Oceanography, Jonas Salk Institute for Biological Studies and University of California, San Diego, La Jolla provides a sympathetic location for the Institute, which conducts pharmaceutical research and development for the pharmaceutical companies of Johnson & Johnson. But the facility's strength lies in its award-winning, L-shaped design, which acknowledges the differences between its two research groups while encouraging them to interact. Chemists, conducting research in a tightly controlled atmosphere safe from such environmental interference as natural light, occupy a compartmentalized environment on the building's southwest side. By contrast, biologists, working under less restrictive conditions, line the building's northeast side in open spaces with outdoor views. The building gives scientists everything else they need, including offices, conference facility and cafeteria, but it puts a lively spin on the proceedings by treating the connection between the two wings as a focal point for social gatherings. Though the sandstone-clad, skylighted, multi-story lobby establishes a boundary between proprietary research areas and public reception, it creates the impression of one continuous space by bringing people together in the lobby at ground level, the conference space on the floor above, and the cafeteria on the floor below.

Top left: Café.
Top right: Reception.
Right: Servery.
Opposite: Lobby.
Photography: David Hewitt/ Anne Garrison.

Carrier Johnson

bkm OfficeWorks
San Diego, California

Even an experienced dealer in high-end office furniture can appreciate how skillfully a professional design firm transforms raw space into a working showroom to display the functional aspects as well as the style and personality of the furniture. San Diego's bkm OfficeWorks illustrates this point superbly in its new, one-story, 13,000-square-foot showroom, designed by Carrier Johnson. The facility's eloquent design vocabulary, complete with dropped ceilings, varying floor patterns and a blend of traditional and contemporary materials, defines distinct areas where intimate furniture mock-ups can be assembled. Yet the space never loses its coherence, due to a neutral color palette that focuses attention on the products, sweeping forms and material changes that create a feeling of energy and movement to pull disparate elements together, and a clear path defined on floor and ceiling to guide visitors. Dealer and designer worked closely together, supported by their long established relationship, to choose furniture and fixtures. Then, Carrier Johnson yielded the purchasing and installation of furnishings to bkm OfficeWorks, letting it take the lead in its area of expertise to streamline the process, save time and money, and demonstrate to visitors the quality they can expect by using its products and services. In other words, the showroom is doing exactly what a showroom is supposed to do.

Top right: Lobby.
Middle right: Hall.
Right: Fabric display.
Opposite: Accent wall.
Photography: Ian White Photography.

Carrier Johnson

Broadway 655
San Diego, California

Above: Elevator lobby.
Right: Exterior.
Bottom right: Lobby.

Photography: Scott McDonald/ Hedrich Blessing.

The first Class-A office tower to be completed in downtown San Diego in more than a decade, Broadway 655, designed by Carrier Johnson, was completed in late 2005. It provides tenants a state-of-the-art, 23-story, 407,000-square-foot office tower with typical floor plates ranging from 20,000-23,000 square feet, energy-saving technology, broadband and fiber optic capabilities, exceptional views and easy access to restaurants, retail shopping, government facilities, residential neighborhoods and the bay front. The building also plays a dynamic role as a physical and visual connector between the city's existing and emerging urban districts, symbolizing San Diego's continuing revitalization even as it honors the existing architectural massing of the surrounding area. Projecting the outward image of a crystalline glass tower rising from a solid base, it reprises its monumental exterior scale inside the lobby with a two-story lobby in travertine-clad walls, granite flooring, and metal paneled ceiling that evokes a museum in its austere grandeur. Outside and in, Broadway 655 is convincing San Diego it was well worth the wait.

CBT

110 Canal Street
Boston, MA 02114-1805
617.262.4354
617.236.0378 (Fax)
www.cbtarchitects.com

CBT

Choate, Hall & Stewart LLP
Boston, Massachusetts

The new offices for this venerable law firm emphasize the prestigious reputation of the firm's practice and the dynamic energy of Boston where the firm was founded some 100 years ago. Conceived as a "lighthouse" that is poised on the top eight floors of Two International Place, the interior spaces are shaped by the tower's unusual circular floor plates. Sparkling light combines with sandy colors and neutral tones that create a pleasing backdrop for views of the harbor, downtown Boston, and the Rose Kennedy Greenway. Playful accents in red, the firm's signature color, are scattered throughout the interior. The offices were organized to foster collabora-

tion, increase efficiency, and provide ample conferencing spaces. Conference rooms and private offices are distributed equally on all floors in order to uphold the firm's synergistic relationship between attorneys and their clients. The Partners' conference center has moveable partitions so that a single large space can be divided into three private rooms. Custom-designed work stations, flexible furniture, and integrated technology help to enhance communication both inside and outside of the firm. The design is governed by a series of contrasts, such as structure and openness, softness and solidity, and dark and light. The reception floor has a do-

mestic quality that provides a warm environment for clients and visitors. Seating areas with cozy leather armchairs are dispersed throughout the open interior. Varied floor treatments, such as carpeting and polished wood, define the individual spaces throughout. A connecting stair blends stone treads with leather-wrapped railings in an elegant, sculptural centerpiece. The open floor plan enhances the intimate quality of the interior spaces and frames the outdoor views. A curved soffit above the conference rooms on the reception floor imitates the curve of the building's exterior envelope. Dark, rich woods serve as a dramatic contrast to the natural light

that floods the interior. Top floor conference rooms feature round windows that are portholes to the outdoors. A cafeteria, known as the "Firm Bite," acts a central gathering place for dining and socializing in a relaxed atmosphere. A lively space, the dining area has gently curved seating and a wall of light poles that use LED technology to fill the room with slowly changing colored hues.

Top left: Reception area and conference room.

Above: Connecting stair.

Opposite bottom right: Multi-purpose room.

Opposite bottom left: Conference room.

Below: Stair detail.

Photography: Anton Grassl.

Bloomberg L.P.
Boston, Massachusetts

CBT provided comprehensive design services for the Boston offices of Bloomberg L.P., the leading global provider of financial data, news, and analysis. This office serves as a news room and conference/training center and includes a TV and radio studio for broadcasting live news reports and interviews. The office enjoys a nearly 360-degree view of Boston from their location in the heart of the Financial District. Daylight and views are preserved through extensive use of glass and open work areas.

Top: Central pantry.

Far left: News room.

Left: Training room.

Bottom far left: Conference room.

Bottom left: Informal meeting space.

Opposite: Reception.

Photography: Anton Grassl.

Office Environments of New England
Boston, Massachusetts

Office Environments of New England is a premier office furniture dealership whose portfolio also includes comprehensive audio/visual and architectural products solutions. CBT designed Office Environments' Boston headquarters, which consists of both showroom and office areas. Diverse design elements were utilized to create defined layers of public, customer interaction space and private staff workspace. The showroom creates a clear and powerful customer experience with an inviting and open café space to meet with clients and a generous display area with specialty lighting and graphics to highlight Office Environments' products. Both formal and informal meeting areas, supported by state-of-the-art technology, are available to accommodate varied meeting styles and requirements.

Top left: Open-plan office.
Top right: Lounge and café.
Left: Reception.
Opposite: Reception.
Photography: Anton Grassl.

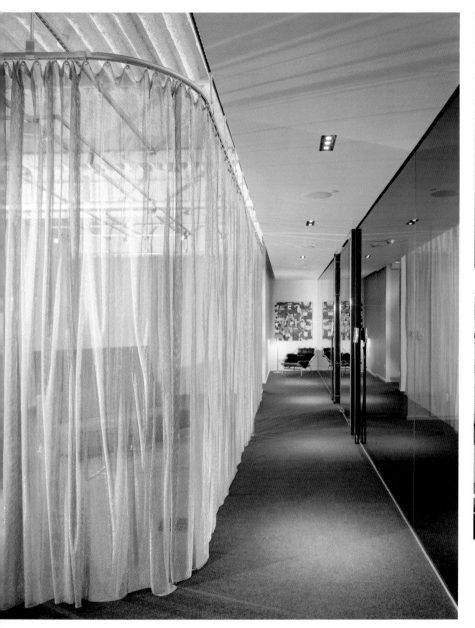

Within the office area, each staff workspace utilizes a universal footprint with furniture components that can be configured to meet the specific needs of each department. A dynamic shared lounge space is centrally-located and provides a social space for staff to interact. A priority for Office Environments was to obtain ample daylight throughout both the showroom and office areas. The design achieves this by providing an open, communicative layout throughout the entire space.

Above: Mockup area.
Top right: Open-plan office.
Middle: Collaborative workspace.
Right: Open-plan workspace.

Champlin/Haupt Architects

424 East Fourth Street
Cincinnati, OH 45202
513.241.4474
513.241.0081 (Fax)
all@charchitects.com
www.charchitects.com

Champlin/Haupt Architects

Ethicon Endo-Surgery, Inc.
Employee Café
Blue Ash, Ohio

Centrally located at Ethicon Endo-Surgery, Inc.'s institute building in Blue Ash, Ohio, the cafeteria is an essential public space in the facility of this Johnson & Johnson company. Prior to renovation, the servery space was congested and outdated. The renovation, designed by Champlin/Haupt Architects, has dramatically improved the space, both functionally and aesthetically, by presenting a fresh and dynamic image the corporation was seeking. The design team took advantage of 17-foot-high ceilings and exterior walls to introduce daylight and views and reshaped the entrance, serving stations and check-out. Renovations also included a new stream-lined circulation flow, placing functional tasks behind the scenes to give cooks more room, and the addition of bold colors, accent lighting, display areas, self-service and control points. "It's not only about creativity and in-novation, but it is also about budget-driven design," says facility manager Rick Cana-van, who is pleased with the architects' effort in meeting the project's budgetary con-straints without compromis-ing design quality. Careful project scheduling even let the cafeteria operate during construction so hundreds of employees never missed a breakfast or lunch.

Top right: Entrance.

Top left: Beverage station/ coffee bar.

Right: Salad bar.

Opposite: Check-out station.

Photography: Greg Matulionis.

Champlin/Haupt Architects

Fifth Third Bank
Madisonville Office Building
Cincinnati, Ohio

Above: Open office area.
Top left: Employee café.
Far left: Exterior with sun screens and fins.
Left: Skylit gallery.
Opposite right: Lobby.
Photography: Dave Brown.

Information Technology

The Fifth Third Bank Madisonville Office Building started life as a 375,000-square-foot warehouse with few windows but lots of 40' high interior space, which served as an inventory center for a national shoe company. The building now houses an award-winning office building for a national bank and has been transformed accordingly into a respectful but contemporary member of the corporate campus. To transform the big box into a viable office with good wayfinding, the design took such actions as installing a second floor in the high bays, introducing daylight through windows and skylights, adding stair towers for egress and interest, and installing fixed aluminum sun shades to control light and articulate facades. Additionally, color palettes were created to identify various departments through carpet, wall colors and signage. For 2,350 employees of this bank holding company serving the Midwest and Florida, the facility provides private and open-plan offices, training rooms, locker rooms, a file room, cafeteria, lunch room, mail room and dock. In order to better serve its 5.5 million customers, Fifth Third chose this centrally located Midwest facility to house a sophisticated data network that works seamlessly with a companion facility on the same campus.

Champlin/Haupt Architects

Shire Pharmaceuticals US, Inc.
Corporate Headquarters
Newport, Kentucky

Above: Lobby/staircase.
Left: Lobby/reception area.
Below left: Board room.
Bottom left: Coffee pantry.
Photography: Greg Matulionis.

Founded in 1986, Shire is one of the world's fastest growing specialty pharmaceutical companies. A new, three-floor, 83,500-square-foot headquarters for 130 employees of Shire Pharmaceuticals US, Inc. in Newport, Kentucky, was designed by Champlin/Haupt Architects. This new corporate headquarters establishes a memorable corporate image that simultaneously unites previously dispersed departments and facilitates internal communication. Distinctive floor plans inspired by the ellipse in the company's logo lend the facility a high level of coherence with a gently curving main circulation corridor. Other activities with their own special spatial orientation include classrooms with video conferencing capabilities and a computer room for international networking. The facility also incorporates private offices, conference and training rooms, laboratory and full kitchen. Open-plan office areas, which occupy the perimeter of linear floor plates, grant everyone spectacular views of downtown Cincinnati and the Ohio River.

Champlin/Haupt Architects

Cinergy
Corporate Headquarters
Cincinnati, Ohio

Perched high above downtown Cincinnati, the corporate headquarters for Cinergy, a provider of energy and energy-related services to customers in Ohio, Kentucky and Indiana, were designed by Champlin/Haupt Architects. The design mirrors the company, appropriately enough, blending traditional architectural details with advanced technology in a two-story, 32,000-square-foot space. Headquarter facilities, including reception space, private offices and conference space for company executives, 30-seat boardroom, dining room, catering kitchen and fitness center promote openness and communication. Private window offices, for example, are enclosed by glazed walls so sunlight and views reach the center of the floor. An internal stair provides speakers an elevated landing for addressing special events in the reception space at the foot of the stairs.

Top right: Hallway to administrative support area.
Top left: Stair lobby at executive offices.
Below left: Executive office.
Right: Board room.
Photography: Robert Ames Cook.

Champlin/Haupt Architects

Cinergy
Power Marketing and Trading Facility
Florence, Kentucky

As a diversified energy company, Cinergy is active in wholesale generation and energy marketing and trading, handling 51.6 billion cubic feet per day of natural gas and 185.1 million megawatt-hours of over-the-counter contracts for the purchase and sale of electricity in 2004. The company's award-winning, two-level, 141,000-square-foot power marketing and trading facility in Florence, Kentucky, designed by Champlin/Haupt Architects, is as sophisticated as the business itself. But the high-profile facility's humble origin catches visitors by surprise. Cinergy had previously used the existing warehouse for company files and maintenance crews. The new and renovated space, including a central, two-story trading room with 120 trading positions, conference center, training room, private executive offices, open administration offices, food service, work-out room and locker rooms, is arrayed on a 116,000-square-foot first floor. A newly added 25,000-square-foot mezzanine features a viewing window at the top of a monumental staircase that allows visitors to observe trading room activity. The sleek new interior design features high-tech systems furniture in the trading room, classic, contemporary furnishings elsewhere, and sophisticated lighting, such as light trough fixtures for traders.

Top right: Lobby/reception area.
Top left: Trading floor.
Middle right: Lounge and stair near staff entrance.
Right: Solarium.
Photography: Tony Schamer.

DMJM Rottet

999 Town & Country Road
Orange, CA 92868
714.571.0900
714.543.0955 (Fax)

3101 Wilson Boulevard
Arlington, VA 22209
703.682.4900
703.682.4901 (Fax)

515 South Flower Street
8th Floor
Los Angeles, CA 90071
213.593.8300
213.593.8610 (Fax)
www.dmjmrottet.com

808 Travis Street
Suite 100
Houston, TX 77002
713.221.1830
713.221.1858 (Fax)

405 Howard Street
4th Floor
San Francisco, CA 94105
415.986.1373
415.986.4886 (Fax)

DMJM Rottet

Haynes Boone, LLP
Houston, Texas

Can an office be a home away from home? The attorneys of Haynes Boone, one of the nation's largest and fastest-growing law firms with over 450 lawyers in 10 offices in the United States, Mexico City and Moscow, regard their offices as workplaces. Yet when rapid growth led the 36-year-old firm to relocate its Houston office to a new, five-floor, 120,000-square-foot space in One Houston Center, a modern downtown high-rise, it acknowledged the long hours lawyers spend at work by developing a cost-effective environment for friendly, collegial encounters as well as highly productive practice. For example, a grand, two-floor conference center limits visitor interaction on typical attorney floors by minimizing the need for conference rooms on individual floors. A relaxed work environment is fostered through such means as corridors on attorney floors that omit end walls to admit views and natural light, and a breakroom off the conference center that offers expansive views of Houston's skyline. Colorful furnishings and an expansive, two-story reception area welcomes visitors and houses the connecting stair between conference center floors. And the firm maintains its reputation for being at the forefront of law firm technology with videoconference rooms, wireless network and scalable technology infrastructure, all of which is subtly integrated in the architecture of the space. Notes Ken Broughton, administrative partner of the firm in Houston, "This space will allow us to continue our strategic expansion and reinforce our firm's position as a leader in the Houston legal and business communities."

Above: Cafe.
Above left: Connecting stair.
Left: Reception & seating.
Opposite top: Internal conference room.
Photography: Bennychan/Fotoworks

DMJM Rottet

Fulbright & Jaworski L.L.P.
Los Angeles, California

In a city where the motion picture industry rules, it's only natural for a law firm to update its public image in relocating a growing practice. The new, three-story, 65,000-square-foot Los Angeles office of Fulbright & Jaworski, designed by DMJM Rottet, represents just such an effort between the prominent, full-service international law firm, with over 950 attorneys in 13 offices, and its designer. Thus, the new facility at City National Plaza, in the heart of the city's financial district, simultaneously supports a modern organization founded in 1919 that strongly believes in the personal relationship between client and attorney and a desire to excel on behalf of the client, and encourages collaboration within the firm. The design abounds in creative details, such as clerestory windows for private window offices and exposed window bays at the ends of floors, letting daylight permeate into internal work areas. An office furniture system shares wood veneers with the office, providing an attractive alternative to millwork administrative stations. But personnel and visitors alike will probably be drawn to such bold spatial gestures as the three-story glass and bronze interconnecting staircase, which allows employees from all floors to meet during the day, and the main reception area and multi-purpose room, where intimate meetings and large events are equally at home. Better yet, the relationships Fulbright & Jaworski wanted to foster in the new workplace began with the development of the project, and are reflected in the design as well as the activities it nurtures.

Above: Reception.

Top left: Conference.

Above left: Administrative workstations.

Left: Staircase detail.

Opposite: Stair.

Photography: Nick Merrick Hedrich Blessing.

DMJM Rottet

Royal Bank of Scotland
Houston, Texas

Founded in Edinburgh by Royal Charter in 1727, the Royal Bank of Scotland has managed to feel quite at home in Houston, having occupied the 60th floor of the JP Morgan Chase Tower for 24 years. So when the bank expanded the Houston office during a recent reorganization that divided it into two departments and required more space and a move to a separate floor, it was delighted to learn it could lease 12,850 square feet on the 65th floor of the prestigious Pei Cobb Freed building. But how do you establish an environment that can maintain the separate identity of two discreet departments while creating a communal space for them to share? The solution for the new facility, designed by DMJM Rottet, places the shared facilities, including conference rooms, visitor offices, reception area, administrative area and an entertaining bar, in a glass "box within a box" shifted off the building grid. The angling of the box is not as arbitrary as it sounds, since the building itself embodies a square floor plan that is chamfered at its southwest corner. The areas within the box are carefully aligned to take advantage of natural light and views of the city landscape, being penetrated by shifting wall planes and transparent materials. To incorporate the identity and heritage of the bank into a space that would be void of

DMJM Rottet

Royal Bank of Scotland
Houston, Texas

decorative motifs, the design uses pattern and grid, as in a tartan plaid, to create texture and interest in the dynamic, planar architecture. It employs an array of building materials, including marble, limestone and birch, modern furnishings and original works of art, as well as a custom striped carpet in the reception area that picks up the royal blue from the bank's logo. The richly layered and superbly detailed composition reflects well on an institution noted for its heritage, solidity, creative strategy and impeccable work. In fact, as employees gather at the entertaining bar every morning to enjoy its panoramic views of Houston, individuals have been heard saying, "I could live like this."

Top: Internal view of main conference with view toward small conference room & entertainment bar.

Above: Reception seating.

Left: Entertaining bar/breakroom.

Francis Cauffman Foley Hoffmann Architects Ltd.

2120 Arch Street
Philadelphia, PA 19103
215.568.8250
215.568.2639 (Fax)
www.fcfh-did.com

Francis Cauffman Foley Hoffmann Architects Ltd.

McNeil Consumer & Specialty Pharmaceuticals
Administration Building B
Fort Washington, Pennsylvania

Right: Individual work area.
Opposite top right: Team touchdown area.
Bottom right: Hub area.
Photography: Don Pearse.

Above: Team room.
Below: Informal team area.

Innovation is a lifeline for established members of the business community facing intensifying global competition. The new workplace project for McNeil Consumer & Specialty Pharmaceuticals at their Fort Washington, Pennsylvania, campus visibly demonstrates the result of a process to transform an existing, traditional, hierarchical workspace into a stimulating and attractive, innovation-oriented environment. First, a detailed strategic workplace study was conducted of the business mission, corporate culture and work processes at McNeil, a Johnson & Johnson company. Then, the design team set out to create an "open and dynamic" space encompassing 49,000 square feet that would encourage greater interaction, collaboration and cross-functional teamwork. McNeil's goal has been achieved by providing a variety of formal and informal work settings, both private and public, to accommodate individual as well as group-oriented, collaborative work. Thus, both onsite and mobile company personnel have a versatile menu of workspaces at their disposal. They include open work stations, private offices, informal team areas, enclosed team rooms of varying sizes, touchdown areas, and a central informal meeting area hub with coffee/copy/mail area and an adjacent conference room. Based on function rather than hierarchy, this aggregation of neighborhoods grouped around central support hubs has drawn such favorable comments as "allows us to meet frequently and more impromptu," "total flexibility to move to different spaces-dock and go," and "the space is more energetic, vibrant."

Francis Cauffman Foley Hoffmann Architects Ltd.

AstraZeneca
Lobby Renovation
Wilmington, Delaware

Francis Cauffman Foley Hoffmann won a design competition at AstraZeneca's U.S. Headquarters in Wilmington, Delaware, to transform an existing empty lobby into a vibrant, multi-use space that expresses the AstraZeneca culture. The resulting renovation, aimed at accommodating informal meetings, plug & play touchdown areas and vendor displays, features a floor plan that divides the lobby into more private zones at the ends with a public zone in the center. There is a retractable partition that partially shelters a section from employee traffic entering and leaving the building through a new secure entrance vestibule. The contemporary interior design incorporates such natural materials as maple wood panels and screens to filter the direct sunlight, granite flooring and colorful textiles. In addition, comfortable lounge seating for casual meetings and ergonomic desk chairs for short intervals of individual touchdown work ties everything together. As a visual image of AstraZeneca, the new space reflects their Swedish heritage through the use of natural daylight, light woods and contemporary furniture, while addressing the aesthetics and functional requirements of a global pharmaceutical company committed to turning ideas into innovative, effective medicines.

Top right: Privacy wall.
Right: Touchdown detail.
Opposite: East view.
Photography: Don Pearse.

Francis Cauffman Foley Hoffmann Architects Ltd.

Fox Rothschild LLP
Doylestown, Pennsylvania

Left: Main conference room.

Below: Lawyers' offices.

Bottom left: Corridor and open area.

Bottom right: Alcove.

Right: Lobby.

Photography: Don Pearse.

Founded in 1907 in Phila-
delphia, Fox Rothschild has
grown to a firm of nearly 300
lawyers practicing in 10 offices located in Pennsylvania,
New Jersey, Delaware, New
York and Florida, making it
one of the nation's 200 largest law firms. Operating with
the resources of a large, full-
service firm, Fox Rothschild
serves clients in conveniently
located offices such as the
new, one-story, 20,000-
square-foot facility for 60
employees in Doylestown,
Pennsylvania. The reloca-
tion of this existing practice
marks its transition from a
Victorian-style environment
to a contemporary one.
Smoothing the transition is
the use of a conventional
"racetrack" floor plan that
positions the centralized
conference center with
private offices along the perimeter in close proximity to
administrative work stations,
the lunch room and other
core functions. In addition,
the spacious reception area,
which receives visitors coming to the conference center,
is handsomely furnished in
fabric-paneled walls, sapele
wood and aluminum trim,
projecting a fresh, timeless
look that befits a law firm
celebrating its first century
in practice.

Francis Cauffman Foley Hoffmann Architects Ltd.

Ethicon, Inc.
Cafeteria and Conference Center
Somerville, New Jersey

For Ethicon, a maker of medical devices that has been a leader in surgical sutures for over a century, the adaptive reuse of a manufacturing plant at its headquarters in Somerville, New Jersey, as a corporate cafeteria and conference center may have seemed unexpectedly familiar. After all, the retrofitting that produced the lively, new 20,000-square-foot facility, designed by Francis Cauffman Foley Hoffmann, represented major surgery for a building. The design incorporates existing high ceilings and generous bays in a cost-effective scheme with new architectural elements, eye-catching colors and creative lighting to satisfy the Johnson & Johnson subsidiary's requirements for dining and conferences. Diners entering the 250-seat cafeteria select their entrées at a bright and airy servery of organically-shaped, island-style serving stations before proceeding to a dining area offering standard or bar height tables and lounge seating. The Conference Center consists of two small conference rooms and a large, dividable conference room. While the Conference Center serves more formal meetings, the cafeteria provides the venue for dining, informal meetings and company-wide town hall meetings. The project is a huge success. It has energized employees who are drawn to the space to eat, meet others and be inspired.

Top right: Business lounge.
Right: Dining area.
Below: Servery entrance.
Photography: Don Pearse.

Gensler

Amsterdam	Denver	Morristown	San Jose
Atlanta	Detroit	New York	San Ramon
Baltimore	Houston	Newport Beach	Seattle
Boston	La Crosse	Northern Virginia	Shanghai
Charlotte	Las Vegas	Phoenix	Tampa
Chicago	London	San Diego	Tokyo
Dallas	Los Angeles	San Francisco	Washington DC

Gensler

Venables, Bell & Partners
San Francisco, California

Against all odds, Paul Venables and Greg Bell, former creative executives at Goodby Silverstein & Partners, and Bob Molineaux, a former Goodby associate partner and managing director at Citron Haligman Bedecarré, count themselves among the rare advertising agency founders who remain friends with a former employer. The trio who started San Francisco's cutting-edge Venables, Bell & Partners not only maintain good relations with Goodby, they leased their first office from them. Now, Venables, Bell continues its unconventional ways—think

of the opera singing golfers in the Barclays Classic—by opening a new, two-story, 13,000-square-foot office for 65 employees, designed by Gensler, overlooking Union Square. What distinguishes this workplace is Venables, Bell's unconventional desire to let clients witness its creative thinking and participate in the process. Accordingly, the design establishes a playful and open environment to match the firm's modus operandi by placing enclosed functions at the core, open-plan areas on the perimeter, transitional spaces wherever needed as multiple-use

areas, and an interior stair in the center to connect the floors and display awards. (Employees call the stair the "tower of power.") The building's shell is treated as a simple, clean envelope of exposed concrete columns and floors to complement a crisp, modern white interior with red accents, where glass, carpet, steel and modern furnishings contrast with suspended plaster coffered ceilings featuring traditional egg-and-dart molding. "The place hums with activity and thought," reports Bell, co-creative director.

Left bottom: Open-plan area.
Right top to bottom: Conference area; Corner in open-plan area; Reception seating; Conference room.

Opposite: Interior stair.
Photography: Nic Lehoux.

90

Gensler

Sun Chemical Corporation
Parsippany, New Jersey

How much color belongs in the workplace? It's a serious issue if you're Sun Chemical Corporation, the U.S. arm of Netherlands-based Sun Chemical Group B.V., the world's largest producer of printing inks and pigments, as well as a leading provider of materials to packaging,

publication, coatings, plastics, cosmetics and other industrial markets. Sun's new three-level, 65,000-square-foot headquarters in Parsippany, New Jersey, designed by Gensler, strikes a lively balance between a colorful environment and a functional workplace. Since Sun's goal was to foster growth and creativity as well as reflect its position in the business world, color displays its power as saturated accents seen against a neutral envelope filled with natural light. Within the reception area, private offices, open-plan areas, board room, conference center, café lounge and cafeteria, occupying the entire fourth floor, part of the second floor and a quadrant of the first floor, strategically located Sun Chemical "Brand Red" lacquered portals mark all entrances and transitional spaces, and strategically located "initiative" walls identify specific business units. Besides these vivid exercises in color application, there are long views to the outdoors framed by architectural openings, clear and translucent glass to layer the interiors and let daylight penetrate deep indoors, six-foot-wide corridors that keep lounges and other amenities visible, and architectural lighting that renders color accurately and enhances textured surfaces. Needless to say, Sun Chemical's pigments and inks are incorporated into architectural finishes throughout the award-winning facility.

Gensler

Brown Rudnick Berlack Israels LLP
New York, New York

For a first-hand look at how a bold, forward-thinking New York law firm should appear, lawyers are calling on Brown Rudnick Berlack Israels in its new, two-level, 44,596-square-foot space at Seven Times Square, designed by Gensler. A Boston-based international law firm founded in 1948 that currently has 200 attorneys serving clients from 10 offices in the United States and Europe, Brown Rudnick shrewdly requested a strong, dynamic presence in Manhattan to expand the practice, attract new talent and build upon its established "brand." The resulting offices, associated support areas, conference center and lunchroom fully exploit the building's geometry as well as its visual command of Broadway, one of New York's most famous thoroughfares. Consequently, all the elements of this unapologetically modern environment form a superbly coordinated whole. These include: the largely open spaces, aggressive architectural forms, spectacular views, state-of-the-art technology, classic modern furniture, sophisticated lighting, modern art collection, and such sleek materials as backpainted glass with stainless steel accents in the elevator lobby, black granite portals with all-glass doors, full-height metal and glass doors and sidelights for private offices, and wood ceilings, marble floors and red lacquer storage units

(bearing Brown Rudnick's signature red) in the conference center. Notes Marilyn Stempler, partner, Brown Rudnick, "Gensler created a dramatic office environment for us that is spacious, bold and very well suited to our clients' expectations."

Top: Reception area.
Above left: Private office.
Above right: Corridor.

Opposite: Conference room.
Photography: Michael Moran.

Gensler

Nokia
Atlanta, Georgia

The Finnish roots of mobile communications leader Nokia are never hard to trace at its state-of-the-art customer service center in Atlanta, thanks to a new, two-story, 18,900-square-foot facility for 100-plus employees, designed by Gensler. The project explores two broad themes, modern technology and the roots of the 141-year-old company and modern architecture in its country of origin, throughout a space comprising a reception area, private and open-plan offices, conference center, control room, data center and computer room. For this reason, the environmental concerns of Finnish Modernism explored by the great Alvar Aalto and his contemporaries are acknowledged with airy, open and naturally-lighted spaces appointed in such basic materials as hardwoods, bamboo flooring, drywall and glass, as well as other environmentally sensitive and/or recycled materials. Numerous details attest to the enthusiasm of the design team such as glass office fronts, a bright color palette, an oval reception desk that resembles a giant log and opens into a sky blue rotunda, a canted glass wall with twigs embedded in it, and a broad ceiling plane of wood that extends from the reception area to the conference and control rooms. While the space rightly focuses on its high-tech central computer room, outfitted with photo-optically lighted racks, and control room, showcasing elaborate video projection systems, it also features gracious public areas with furnishings designed by Aalto. Savoring the ambiance, numerous visitors praise the design because "It feels just like Finland."

Top left: General office area.

Top right: Reception.

Above: Control room.

Photography: Sherman Takata/ Gensler.

Gerner Kronick + Valcarcel, Architects, PC

443 Park Avenue South
New York, NY 10016
212.679.6362
212.679.5877 (Fax)
www.gkvarchitects.com

Gerner Kronick + Valcarcel, Architects, PC

PB Capital Corporation
New York, New York

Here's a challenging contemporary design problem: Can you provide enough space to assemble an office's entire staff without wasting floor area for an infrequently used facility? While you're at it, can you create a dynamic entry for hosting informal meetings in lieu of a formal reception area, since visitors are few? These questions have shaped the lively, new Manhattan office of PB Capital Corporation, a New York-based subsidiary of Deutsche Postbank AG founded in 1976 that is active in commercial real estate lending and the corporate bond and loan markets. The firm's two-floor, 45,000-square-foot facility, designed by Gerner Kronick + Valcarcel, Architects, gives 80 employees an innovative solution within a modern environment appointed in terrazzo, stainless steel, maple wood, glass, carpet tile and European furnishings. By placing the board room adjacent to the entry "hang out" space and separating them with two eight-foot-wide doors, one pivot and one sliding, the two areas can function as one. Thus, at the heart of a traditional configuration of private window offices, core work stations, lounges, internal stair, pantries and restrooms, a big gathering space can appear and disappear with the speed of the financial world.

Above: Private offices.
Left Informal gathering space.
Lower left: Boardroom.
Opposite: Entry and informal gathering space.
Photography: Paul Warchol.

Gerner Kronick + Valcarcel, Architects, PC

Sonnenschein Nath & Rosenthal LLP
New York, New York

Sonnenschein Nath & Rosenthal, a 700-attorney, global law firm founded in 1906, is noted for its innovative legal services, attending to corporate and institutional clients through integrated, inter-office cooperation and teamwork among practice groups. Though it realized its new, four-story, 160,000-square-foot midtown Manhattan office, designed by Gerner Kronick + Valcarcel, Architects, could not possibly convey the full extent of its activities in one glance, it wanted visitors to sense its overall breadth at the entry to a "warm yet sophisticated" environment. Accordingly, the modern space incorporates some dramatic flourishes within an otherwise traditional law office scheme that comprises a reception area, private and open offices, conference center, internal stair, lunchroom, warming pantry, restrooms and support spaces. The design features sleek interiors of Eucalyptus wood panels, travertine floors, indirect lighting, glass and glass plank bridge that revolve around an airy, two-story atrium that visitors view from the top upon arriving. New Yorkers may pride themselves on having seen everything, but the atrium and the office rarely fail to draw visitors' admiration.

Top right: Stairway.
Middle: Reception.
Above: Conference room.

Right: Lunch room.
Opposite: Reception.
Photography: Adrian Wilson.

Gerner Kronick + Valcarcel, Architects, PC

Pershing Square Capital Management
New York, New York

Right: Private offices.

Below: Entry and elevator lobby.

Bottom: Corridor to conference rooms.

Opposite: Conference room with Turbine (wall) and Ejector Seat (freestanding).

Photography: Adrian Wilson.

New Yorkers would kill for the panoramic views of Central Park that are enjoyed by the 15 employees of Pershing Square Capital Management who occupy its new, one-floor, 10,000-square-foot office, designed by Gerner Kronick + Valcarcel, Architects. Of course, no one had to be told about the value of this amenity, and the design of the space, encompassing a waiting room, private offices, secretarial work stations, conference rooms, open trading area with bar area, gym and restrooms, fully reflects this. To share the views as widely as possible, the design uses fully glazed office fronts, high ceilings, and a sensuous circulation spine separating public and private spaces to let daylight and views penetrate deep into the space. Employees of Pershing Square, a hedge fund that made headlines recently by proposing that McDonald's Corporation restructure itself, and their visitors can easily be forgiven for thinking that the views nearly overwhelm the office. Fortunately, anyone who turns away from the windows soon discovers that the spare, modern space, graced by fine furnishings and original artwork, is quite satisfying in its own right.

102

Gerner Kronick + Valcarcel, Architects, PC

Cleary Gottlieb Steen & Hamilton LLP
Midtown Conference Center
New York, New York

Conference centers are valuable assets to law firms, whose ability to conduct large, complex and demanding negotiations can be critical to their success. For the New York office of Cleary Gottlieb Steen & Hamilton, a leading international law firm with some 850 attorneys at 12 closely integrated offices in major financial centers around the world, a new, one-floor, 8,500-square-foot midtown conference center, designed by Gerner Kronick + Valcarcel, Architects, is a good example. The facility contains a reception area, private offices, secretarial work stations, servery, warming pantry, IT room, support areas and restrooms, in addition to conference rooms. Since it captures views of Central Park and midtown Manhattan, Cleary Gottlieb has developed a clean, precise and minimal modern interior as a foil. The design does indeed yield to the views, but it has a spare elegance of its own. Featured in a handsome interior of figured sycamore, bronze trim, carpet and stone are state-of-the-art conference rooms with electrified glass that is transparent when energized, transmitting daylight and views that instantly turn opaque white when the current is off.

Above left: Conference room.
Right top to bottom: Office; lobby; lobby at night; servery.
Photography: Adrian Wilson.

104

H. Hendy Associates

4770 Campus Drive
Suite 100
Newport Beach, CA 92660
949.851.3080
949.851.0807 (Fax)
www.hhendy.com

H. Hendy Associates

Major Financial Institution
Training Center
Rolling Meadows, Illinois

Right: Hands-on training area.
Below right: Training room entry.
Bottom right: Touchdown area.
Below: Trophy case ante area.
Opposite: Coffe bar.
Photography: Craig Dugan/ Hedrich Blessing.

Anyone who visits traditional training facilities can describe how uncomfortable and stifling they are. For this reason, a major financial institution took a decidedly different approach in its new, one-story, 11,000-square-foot training facility for 135 employees in Rolling Meadows, Illinois, designed by H. Hendy Associates. The design, incorporating a reception area, training rooms, break-out areas, lunch room/coffee bar and restrooms in an existing office building, anticipates the trainees' experience with environments that support them through hours of intensive training. Its assured handling of spaces begins when trainees enter the reception area, a gracious, open space, and the adjacent trophy case room, an inspiring display of the institution's history. Similar attention to detail is visible in such varied settings as break-away areas where trainees can contact their home offices, a casual meeting and eating area featuring banquette seating, and large picture windows, and perimeter spaces with nearly floor-to-ceiling windows, open ceilings, and ceiling-mounted heaters to compensate for harsh Midwestern winters. Not only do spaces offer easy wayfinding and convenient access to technology, they provide comfort and style, thanks to hip, contemporary furnishings. Indeed, executives have praised the facility since opening day, and trainees say they feel "right at home."

H. Hendy Associates

Corporate Synergies Group
Mt. Laurel, New Jersey

Corporate Synergies is known as an innovative employee benefits brokerage and consulting firm offering comprehensive benefit solutions at competitive carrier rates. Its new, one-floor, 40,000-square-foot office for 180 employees in Mt. Laurel, New Jersey, surprises visitors by demonstrating that CEO Eric Raymond is a passionate philanthropist, globe-traveling photographer and advocate for endangered species. The open environment, designed by H. Hendy Associates, fills a former warehouse with a reception area, private offices, open work areas, training center, art gallery, lunchroom, open coffee bar and server room. The space is the result of just five accelerated months of design, demolition and construction. The new facility overcomes obstacles from its previous life by concealing large, weight-bearing columns within heavily massed walls with strategically placed cut-outs, closing off harsh industrial skylights and enlarging existing exterior windows, and introducing a setting inspired by Raymond's global travels, with marble, exotic woods, saturated earth tones, tribal artifacts, photography by the CEO, and contemporary furnishings. Expressing his satisfaction with the design, Raymond explains, "We chose H. Hendy Associates because we were confident they could design and construct a building that embodied our culture, was flexible enough to accommodate future growth, and complete it on time."

Top right: Hallway.
Top left: Reception desk.
Left: Art gallery.
Opposite: Guest seating in reception area.
Photography: Craig Dugan/ Hedrich Blessing.

H. Hendy Associates

Herman Miller Showroom
Costa Mesa, California

Devoid of people and activity, too many furniture showrooms inhibit customers from comprehending how their employees would interact with the products on display. By contrast, Workplace Resource, a Herman Miller dealer in Costa Mesa, California, has deliberately developed a one-floor, 13,600-square-foot working showroom where its employees use the products of this renowned office and residential furniture manufacturer daily. The space, designed by H. Hendy Associates, blends function and design in a variety of "zones" where the different product lines, styles, colors and finishes support the Herman Miller sales process in a manner that appears seamless to customers. To accomplish this, the design team extends design motifs used in the "hosting zone" throughout the facility, incorporating architectural elements such as panels, frame-and-tile, poles and mobile graphics to maintain customers' interest. Anne Alex, president of Workplace Resource, is pleased to report, "When people step off the elevator, the typical response is 'Wow. Something is different here.' That awe factor is exactly what we wanted to create, and what we wanted to show our clients that they can also create." She proudly adds that the average furniture showroom visit is half an hour, but clients spend an average of two hours with Herman Miller here.

Top left: Product zone.
Below left: Discovery zone 2.
Bottom: Elevator lobby/ reception area.
Below: Sales area.
Opposite: Hosting zone.
Photography: Milroy McAleer.

H. Hendy Associates

L.A.R.D. Investments, L.P.
Santa Fe Springs, California

In designing L.A.R.D. Investment's 18,000-square-foot office in Santa Fe Springs, Calif., H. Hendy Associates has done more than achieve the warm and inviting atmosphere for employees and visiting CEOs as identified in an in-depth discovery process with the client. The team of expert designers also masterfully blended the décor to match the partners' unique tastes.

The reception area, private offices, executive boardroom, open office space and gallery boast gorgeous shades of rust, yellow ochre and gold. Multi-colored slate, walls covered in fabric, lustrous hardwood floors, streamlined glass partitions for the work stations and contemporary office furniture add to the executive chic feel. The one-story layout is in keeping with the company's

dedication to compartmentalizing departments while maintaining an "open-air" feel of sharing information and amenities.

An impressive feat of the design team is the gallery, a 110-foot-long corridor-turned-showcase for displaying the history of the company. "Our environment enhances our associates ability to perform their job everything has its place. Walking through the space you have the feeling I would love to work here." said David Flores, vice president of L.A.R.D. Investments.

Top right: Board room.
Top left: Gallery.
Right: Reception area.
Photography: Paul Bielenberg.

JPC Architects

601 108th Avenue NE
Suite 2250
Bellevue, WA 98004
425.641.9200
425.637.8200 (Fax)
www.jpcarchitects.com

JPC Architects

Gas Powered Games
Redmond, Washington

A monumental castle wall, shimmering in its metallic finish beneath a ceiling of exposed metal decking, greets visitors in the reception area of Gas Powered Games, a computer game developer in Redmond, Washington. Gamers know this "castle" as an icon of company founder Chris Taylor's 2002 inaugural title, Dungeon Siege, an epochal 3D role-playing game. But it's obvious even to the uninitiated guest touring the new, one-level, 26,000- square-foot office, designed by JPC Architects, that the 150-plus employees occupy a unique environment that reflects their game products and supports the job tasks in their programming studio. Thus, the playful spirit of the reception area extends to the monitor-focused studio, where low lighting levels are offset by theater walkway lighting and boldly patterned carpet tiles. Conference rooms can be combined with lunch and collabora- tion spaces by rolling up firehouse-style aluminum and glass doors.

Top right: Reception area display.
Right: Programming studio.
Below: Conference area.
Opposite: Reception area.
Photography: Ben Benschneider.

JPC Architects

Chempoint.com
Bellevue, Washington

Chempoint.com is not your conventional business. To emphasize its philosophy, North America's leading "e-distributor" of specialty and fine chemical products and services, founded in 1999 by Univar, a major global distributor of chemicals, has developed a new suburban Seattle office for 75 employees that is hardly conventional either. The 23,000-square-foot facility, designed by JPC Architects, focuses on an open "village green" to define the workplace and encourage internal communication. The "green," encircled by conference rooms with large sliding glass doors, lunchroom and bistro, dominates the mostly open office environment. The reception station is set off by a backdrop of shimmering chain mail screening a mail/copy room. Other office components such as the teaming rooms, break-out lounges, individual work stations and private offices are handled with equal care.

Above: Village Green.
Right: Teaming room.
Opposite top: Reception area.
Opposite bottom: Bistro.
Photography: Ben Benschneider.

JPC Architects

Wizards of the Coast
Renton, Washington

Enthusiastic customers of Wizards of the Coast, a subsidiary of Hasbro that develops and publishes trading card games, tabletop role-playing games, novels, magazines, family card and board games, and electronic media products might wonder why its products originated in a space once described as a "sea of cubical workstations." Now, JPC Architects has designed a new, four-story, 90,000-square-foot office for 300 "wizards" in Renton, Washington that opens up the cubicles with break-out and informal meeting areas, hard-walled offices and circulation paths to teaming nodes. The new office, comprising a reception area, private and open office groupings, conference facilities, lunchroom, data center and features an orb-shaped core with radiant avenues that open into various "neighborhoods" or studios. There's even room for character displays along the orb's elliptical path to heartily welcome the "wizards" to their new home.

Top: Gallery.
Far left: Office "neighborhood."
Left: Character display.
Opposite: Reception.
Photography: Ben Benschneider.

JPC Architects

Greenpoint Technologies
Kirkland, Washington

When corporate jet owners are ready to order custom interiors for their Boeing aircraft, clients as diverse as Saudi Arabian Royalty and the White House turn to Greenpoint Technologies, an aviation interior design firm founded in 1988. Given its prominence as a preferred OEM supplier to the Boeing Company, Greenpoint recently asked JPC Architects to create an appropriate environment to showcase its design focus to its exclusive, high-powered clientele. The new, 35,000-square-foot facility, which houses a reception area, executive offices, conference rooms, boardroom, break rooms, design studio, gallery and café, meets these objectives with an environment that acts as a creative framework for displaying the level of detail Greenpoint achieves in its work. Subtle references to jet cabin interiors, such as indirect lighting and a round oculus above the reception area illuminated to represent the sky seen from the cabin at 35,000 feet.

Kling

2301 Chestnut Street
Philadelphia, PA 19103
215.569.5277
215.569.5284 (Fax)
www.kling.us

Kling

AstraZeneca
Federal Government Affairs Office
Washington, D.C.

Left: View of reception/lobby from corridor.

Right: Reception/lobby and boardroom.

Bottom left: View of pantry/café.

Below: Private offices and support staff work stations.

Photography: Tom Crane and Jeffrey Totaro.

AstraZeneca, a leading global pharmaceutical company with $21.4 billion dollars in sales (2004), fights diseases in such vital areas of medical need as cancer, cardiovascular, gastrointestinal, infection, neuroscience and respiratory with medicines that are noted for innovation and effectiveness. So when the company recently developed a one-level, 10,000-square foot Federal Government Affairs Office, designed by Kling, to house its lobbying activities in Washington, D.C., it relied on creativity and pragmatism as well. The modern interiors include private offices lining the building perimeter, lobby, boardroom, work stations, pantry/café and miscellaneous support spaces at the building interior. Clear glass lets daylight penetrate deep inside through private office fronts and dramatizes the entrance on the multi-tenant floor. Higher-end finishes and furniture, employed in public areas for maximum impact, are balanced by more utilitarian furnishings in work areas, following established corporate standards. Despite its monumentality, the reception space is flexible enough so large-scale, after-hour events can flow into the adjacent boardroom, helping a company founded in 1913 to be prepared for whatever 21st-century business requires.

Kling

In light of rapidly developing digital technologies the medical world is rethinking the way it shares information about research and development. Elsevier, the medical publishing subsidiary of Reed Elsevier and a world leader with 73 locations, 7,000 employees and over 20,000 products and services, has opened a new regional headquarters in Philadelphia, designed by Kling, that completely reverses its traditional image. The five-floor, 125,000-square foot space, which relocates Elsevier from the historical publishing community in Washington Square to a contemporary, Center City high-rise, is deliberately aimed at a younger, more technologically savvy employee. Its workplace environment, based on benchmarking tools and demographic studies, estab-lishes such new concepts as teaming "neighborhoods," collaborative spaces, video conferencing, casual and formal meeting spaces, inter-active reception lobby with product display, and even a hip cyber café. With open perimeter planning, glass private office fronts, and modular work stations, Elsevier now offers a light-filled, flexible and commu-nicative space that keeps it on the forefront of medical publishing.

Top right: Casual meeting spaces.

Right: Cyber café.

Below: Reception/lobby.

Opposite: Elevator lobby.

Photography: Tom Crane and Jeffrey Totaro.

Kling

Although nobody doubts Turner is one of the world's largest construction companies with over 5,000 employees handling projects valued at $7 billion in 2004, the industry powerhouse is eager to remain a builder of tenant fit-outs and other small projects. In fact, the new, one-story, 30,000-square foot Philadelphia headquarters of Turner's Special Projects Group, designed by Kling and managed and built by Turner, intentionally highlights the two firms' small-scale capabilities. A new corporate planning module combining private offices and open-plan work stations has produced a flexible, integrated environment where even specialized requirements, such as work stations for large, 36-inch x 48-inch drawing sheets, fit cohesively. Materials and furnishings are also handled imaginatively to create a "refined industrial" aesthetic that reflects Turner's passion for building. The main conference room, for example, is entered through a wall of full-height, sandblasted glass doors that pivot so space flows uninterrupted for business and social events. Even private offices and conference rooms at the perimeter enjoy such distinctive features as doorways of corrugated metal siding. For prospective clients, Turner and Kling now have dazzling proof that small is beautiful.

Above: Reception/lobby.

Top left: Private office.

Top far left: Detail of conference.

Left: Open plan work stations.
Opposite right: Conference room table with removeable top over pool table.

Photography: Tom Crane and Jeffrey Totaro.

Kling

Pepper Hamilton LLP
Wilmington, Delaware

The establishment of a one-level, 19,000-square foot branch office in Wilmington, Delaware provides a highly visible presence for Pepper Hamilton, a multi-practice, Philadelphia-based law firm of 400 lawyers and 10 offices. The offices are located in what is often called the corporate capital of the world. The new office, designed by Kling, allows the firm to simultaneously embrace the city's culture and its own 116-year-old heritage through a traditional style environment featuring stone flooring, Oriental rugs, wood-paneled walls, coffered ceilings, fine furnishings and

advanced technology. Perhaps the space that best illustrates the firm's capabilities is the central Conference Center, adjacent to the main reception area. Its large, divisible conference rooms, caucus rooms and video conference rooms with integrated power and data plus the latest AV gear, are equipped to handle such wide-ranging issues as corporate and commercial law, banking and financial services, creditors' rights and bankruptcy, intellectual property and computer law, real estate, venture capital, corporate and commercial litigation and alternative dispute resolution. The result is a win-win for all:

world-class services for clients and a collegial, "boutique" firm atmosphere for 15 lawyers and their support staff.

Above: Reception room.
Top right: Lunchroom.
Above right: Reception/lobby.
Right: Boardroom.
Photography: Tom Crane and Jeffrey Totaro.

Margulies & Associates

234 Congress Street
Sixth Floor
Boston, MA 02110
617.482.3232
617.482.0374 (Fax)
www.margulies.com

Margulies & Associates

Northland Investment Corporation
Newton, Massachusetts

Right: Reception/lobby.

Below right: Lobby landing and main entrance.

Below: Exterior.

Opposite: Lobby stairway.

Photography: Warren Patterson.

Curb appeal speaks volumes about a building and its occupants, as real estate professionals know. So when Northland Investment Corporation recently retained Margulies & Associates to renovate 2,500 square feet of its three-story, 27,000-square-foot corporate office for 40 employees in Newton, a Boston suburb, covering the main entrance, lobby and selected office interiors, it sought curb appeal. Specifically, it requested a visual presence befitting a leading real estate operating company founded in 1970 that currently holds a $1.3-billion portfolio of 60 properties encompassing some 14 million square feet. The result is a 1980s office building displaying a contemporary sense of style, highlighted by a bold, new sense of transparency between indoors and outdoors. With sleek architectural detailing incorporating such contemporary materials and finishes as steamed European beech paneling, stainless steel, frosted glass, French limestone floors and decorative sconces, Northland Investment's office environment appears dramatically larger in scale and importance. That's curb appeal.

Margulies & Associates

eSecLending
Boston, Massachusetts

Sometimes the right move for a young, growing company takes it to an existing facility, where private offices, partitions, woodwork and lighting are adapted to new uses quickly and economically. That's the logic behind eSecLending's new, one-floor, 14,000-square-foot office in Boston, designed by Margulies & Associates. Twenty employees of eSecLending, a division of Old Mutual PLC that is the securities industry's leading manager and administrator of exclusive securities lending arrangements, were housed in Old Mutual offices atop the John Hancock tower in Boston's Back Bay.

Yearning for its own space and identity, eSecLending leased a vacated office in the Financial District. Margulies & Associates saved time and money with high-impact complementary finishes and furnishings that established the company's image and culture in the reception area, trading floor, conference room and private offices. "Margulies exceeded our expectation," reports Karen O'Connor, eSecLending's CFO, "with a design that created a stunning space with functional workspaces."

Above: Reception.

Opposite top left: Reception with view of conference room.

Opposite bottom left: Conference room.

Photography: Lynne Damianos.

Margulies & Associates

The Coyle Company
Waltham, Massachusetts

Above: Open-plan work station.
Left: Conference room.
Below left: Private office.
Bottom left: Lunchroom/kitchen.
Opposite: Reception.
Photography: Warren Patterson.

Focusing exclusively on estate and generational planning for affluent clients since 1981 has enabled The Coyle Company to become a respected financial services firm. The company has a national reputation for integrity, discretion, diligent service and trustworthy management of the estates of individuals with a minimum net worth of $20 million. For this reason, Coyle's new, single-level, 5,000-square-foot office for 15 employees in Waltham, Massachusetts, designed by Margulies & Associates, establishes a private and reassuring classic setting of marble, carpet, textiles, glass, wood veneer, original artwork, pendant and decorative lighting fixtures and comfortable furniture. In this professional environment of private offices, conference rooms, and a lunchroom surrounding a reception area and open-plan work stations, visitors can freely discuss sensitive financial matters with members of Coyle's professional team. Janet Coyle, president of The Coyle Company, happily declares, "There is such a great sense of color and proportion in the design of the space."

Margulies & Associates

The State Room
Boston, Massachusetts

Left: Harborside Salons.
Below left: Reception.
Bottom left: Window wall view
of Harborside Salons.

Photography: Daniel Doke.

Boston looks so splendid from the 33rd floor of 60 State Street, a modern skyscraper surrounded by such 18th-century icons as the Old State House, Faneuil Hall and Quincy Market, that The State Room, a new premier special event venue sharing the floor with the Boston University Club, wisely gives the views starring roles in its facility. Thus, when Longwood Events took over a space formerly operated as the Bay Tower Room and retained Margulies & Associates to design a 5,800-square-foot renovation, it realized an architecture of understated elegance was required. Indeed, the new accommodations, comprising the reception area, coat check, bar, sales and administrative offices, and two event rooms, Haborside Salon Three (1,198 square feet) and Harborside Salon Four (2,069 square feet), offer an uncommonly refined, luxurious and versatile framework for viewing Boston. Elegance is everywhere, in the reception area's concentric elliptical ceiling soffits, tiny, star-like glass lights and Italian chandelier of hand-blown crystal, in the Salons' semi-translucent ceiling of undulating waves, and such materials as hardwood floors, glass tiles, glass bead wall coverings, silk drapes and Bauhaus-style modern furnishings. Surveying the outcome, Alina Apteker, owner of Longwood Events, concludes, "Margulies & Associates delighted us with a very creative solution."

McCarthy Nordburg, Ltd.

3333 East Camelback Road
Suite 180
Phoenix, AZ 85018
602.955.4499
602.955.4599 (Fax)
www.mccarthynordburg.com

McCarthy Nordburg, Ltd.

Pulte Homes, Inc.
Regional Offices
Scottsdale, Arizona

If only Frank Lloyd Wright could see it now. Record population growth in the resort community of Scottsdale, Arizona, where the Genius of the Prairie built Taliesin West in 1937, has fueled the expansion of numerous businesses serving metropolitan Phoenix, including the regional operations of Pulte Homes, a leading homebuilder active in 27 states. To manage expanding sales to first-time, move-up and active adult homebuyers in the region, the Bloomfield Hills, Michigan-based Fortune 150 company recently completed new, three-floor, 150,000-square-foot Regional Offices for 600 employees, designed by McCarthy Nordburg. The facility, which houses a lobby and building common areas, private offices, open work stations, conference and training rooms, call center, lunch room and bistro, as well as mortgage and title entities, streamlines operations by consolidating departments and anticipates future growth and reorganization with flexible space planning and universal design. Equally important is the design's role in portraying Pulte as a professional homebuilder that believes home building should change as people's needs change.

Thus, Pulte's new workplace is a largely open and finely detailed space of warm earth tones, such traditional materials as stone, mosaics, metal, Venetian stucco and cast glass, and comfortable, residential-style furnishings. Its resemblance to an old Tuscan home is a subtle reminder that there's a place for Old World charm even in modern life, a message Scottsdale's 234,900 residents and 7.4 million annual visitors can gladly endorse.

Top left: Conference room doorway.

Above: Lobby.

Opposite bottom right: Stained glass.

Opposite bottom left: Lobby and reception desk.

Photography: Michael Norton/ Norton Photography, Inc.

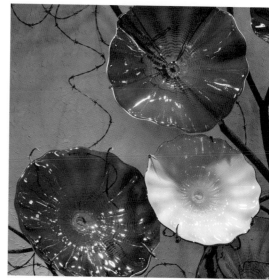

McCarthy Nordburg, Ltd.

Waste Management, Inc.
Western Regional Headquarters
Scottsdale, Arizona

A strong design based on simple lines, basic materials and a traditional office layout forms the heart of the Scottsdale, Arizona office of Waste Management, North America's leading provider of comprehensive waste and environmental services. It's not surprising that the new, one-floor, 25,000-square-foot facility for 65 employees, designed by McCarthy Nordburg, gets down to business with a minimum of fuss. After all, Houston-based Waste Management wants its workplaces to promote the practice of inclusive management, the creation of a high performing environment, and the presence of a local connection to superior service, all within the context of prevailing tenant improvement allowances. The Western Regional Headquarters makes a virtue of its modest budget through a design solution that incorporates simplified, angular forms, masses of color and contrasts and positive/negative recesses with lighting enhancement. Not only are the lobby, private offices, open office areas, conference rooms, training rooms and

lunch room both functional and attractive, the lobby is strategically arranged to project a compelling image that visitors notice immediately upon arriving. In fact, the completed construction, which incorporates white maple and dark cherry veneers, granite, limestone, stainless steel and glass, is not unlike Waste Management's ongoing effort to promote the wise re-use of materials in a society that now recognizes its far-reaching impact on planet earth.

Top: Lobby and reception desk.
Above: Seating group in lobby.
Opposite: Detail of lobby wall.

Photography: Michael Norton/ Norton Photography, Inc.

McCarthy Nordburg, Ltd.

**Opus West Corporation
Regional Headquarters**
Phoenix, Arizona

Were the proverbial shoemaker to reconsider his children's footwear in today's market-driven economy, he would surely give them dazzling examples of their father's art to demonstrate all over town. By contrast, Opus West Corporation never hesitated to exploit the marketing potential of its new Regional Headquarters in Phoenix. The new, one-story, 21,000-square-foot space for 90 employees, designed by McCarthy Nordburg, is both an effective work environment and a showcase profiling this major real estate developer's technical skills and commitment to quality. Aside from being one of hundreds of design-build and tenant improvement projects that McCarthy Nordburg has designed for Opus West, the Regional Headquarters gave the design firm the opportunity to work closely with its long-term client, carefully studying every aspect of the design, from the stone flooring to the ceiling planes and lighting. Millwork and paneling, display niches, integrated and illuminated signage were all detailed to perfect the integration of materials, detailing and workmanship. For established and prospective customers, the superb function, fit and finish of the facility, featuring a lobby with a narrative history wall displaying the company's awards and heritage along with private offices, open offices, conference rooms and lunch room, is a convincing demonstration of why Opus West has been involved in developing over 16 million square feet of office, industrial and retail space throughout the West since its founding in 1979.

Top left: Display area in lobby.
Top right: Conference room.
Right: Lobby.
Opposite: Reception desk.
Photography: Michael Norton/ Norton Photography, Inc.

McCarthy Nordburg, Ltd.

Carl T. Hayden Veterans Affairs Medical Center Ambulatory Care Clinic Addition
Phoenix, Arizona

Knowing how to be tough and compassionate at the same time is a gift the best health care institutions perform so effortlessly the public may not realize how difficult it is. The new, two-story, 76,650-square-foot Ambulatory Care Clinic addition to the 132-bed Carl T. Hayden Veterans Affairs Medical Center, in Phoenix, was designed by Anderson Debartolo and Pan/Fluor Daniel with interiors designed by McCarthy Nordburg. The addition faces high traffic flow that calls for low-maintenance materials, but turns a compassionate face to visitors because of the diversity of the population likely to enter the facility. The Clinic, which consists of primary care clinics, medical and surgical specialty clinics and space for other clinical functions, has been designed as a healing environment that supports the needs of patients and staff, as well as an example of good wayfinding providing a straightforward circulation plan and strategically placed landmarks. The contemporary interiors, appointed in such durable yet attractive materials as terrazzo flooring, maple wood, brushed stainless steel and opaque glass, gives the Hayden VA Medical Center a fresh, contemporary look filled with natural light beginning right at the entrance, where a canopied maple reception desk in opaque glass and a geometric feature wall greet visitors. While the design cannot entirely alleviate the anxieties and discomforts of patients, it goes a long way towards making ambulatory care more accessible.

Top left: Corridor.
Top right: Main entrance.
Right: Corridor.
Photography: Jim Christy/ Jim Christy Studio

Mojo•Stumer Associates, P.C.

14 Plaza Road
Greenvale, NY 11548
516.625.3344
516.625.3418 (Fax)
www.MOJOSTUMER.com

Mojo•Stumer Associates, P.C.

Prentice Capital Management LP
New York, New York

A New York-based money management organization with over $1 billion under management, primarily in the retail/consumer sector, Prentice Capital Management is young, forward-thinking and willing to roll up its sleeves as an active investor in such companies as Wet Seal, KB Toys and Goodys Family Clothing, where it owns significant stakes. What kind of work environment would best suit its 40 employees? The optimum solution for Prentice turns out to be a one-story, 17,000-square-foot facility, designed by Mojo•Stumer Associates, that is decidedly corporate in tone, yet reflects the firm's lively and modern style. The configuration of the office follows the standard layout of the corporate world, featuring private offices and conference rooms on the perimeter, open-plan work stations in the interior, along

Above: Seating group in reception.

Top left: View of reception area from elevator lobby.

Left: Reception desk detail.

Bottom left: Elevator lobby.

Opposite: Reception area.

Photography: Elliot Kaufman.

Mojo•Stumer Associates, P.C.

with a reception area, lunch room and kitchen. However, there are also a gym, recreation area and lounge for employees, acknowledging the benefits of recreation, relaxation and social interaction as a counterpoint to the demands of work in the financial world. The look of the office recognizes the need for balance as well. Although it began as an exercise in minimalism, it developed into a more nuanced image with the development of complex architectural forms, the selection of soft, monochromatic earth tones, such warm and timeless materials as wood, stone, stainless steel and black painted metal, and stylish contemporary furnishings, and the installation of a sophisticated lighting system that gives special attention to the firm's large photography

Top: Conference room.
Above: Executive office.
Opposite: Corrider.

Mojo•Stumer Associates, P.C.

collection. With the space said to "fit like a glove," Prentice is highly satisfied with its investment in its own people and operations.

Top left: Restroom.
Top right: View of Chrysler Building.
Above right: Kitchen.
Right: Traders' desks.

NELSON

The NELSON Building
222-30 Walnut Street
Philadelphia, PA 19106
215.925.6562
215.925.9151 (Fax)
www.nelsononline.com

NELSON

Hennepin County Brookdale Regional Center
Brooklyn Center, Minnesota

Despite global concern about the limits of growth, bigger can still be better, even in government. To improve public services for many of its 1.2 million residents, Minnesota's Hennepin County recently completed a remodeling and expansion of Brookdale Regional Center, in Brooklyn Center, designed by NELSON in collaboration with Buetow & Associates, architect of record, and Abraham & Associates, associate architect, that has doubled the existing facility to 135,000 square feet. Yet the space feels more accessible and inviting than ever. People in the northern part of the county served by Brookdale can now enter one of two rotundas to stroll along an enclosed pedestrian arcade that connects them to general services, library, district courts, community corrections, public defender, sheriff, economic, property, children, adult and family services. Among the facility's highlights are the Brookdale Area Library, featuring expanded storage for its collections and over 100 computer workstations, the Brookdale District Court, displaying an enlarged courtroom and more spacious public waiting areas, and the Brookdale Service Center, offering an automated customer queuing management system and twice as many service stations, plus such amenities as community meeting spaces, doubled parking capacity, and, fulfilling the arcade's image as "Main Street," a lively little café.

Top left: Sculpture on display.
Top right: Corridor at information desk.
Middle right: Cobalt Café.
Bottom right: Service desk.
Opposite: Rotunda.
Photography: Copyright Dana Wheelock, Wheelock Photography.

NELSON

Financial Institution Call Center
East Providence, Rhode Island

Like Cinderella, a former costume jewelry factory in East Providence, Rhode Island has been transformed into a jewel in the crown of a Financial Institution, thanks to a makeover that has produced a new, two-level, 175,000-square-foot call center for 1,200 employees. Part of the Institution's commitment to maintain jobs in a region where it merged with an existing entity, the new facility focuses on speed to market and attracting top talent. A collaborative design by NELSON's offices in New York, Philadelphia, Boston and Tampa has placed four call center units of team workstations, conference rooms and support areas on the nearly 140,000-square-foot main level and such employee amenities as a cafeteria, game room

and fitness center on the lower level. Pragmatic as the design is, it never compromises its occupants. Its vast, new floor plan, for example, is divided into manageable quadrants with core facilities optimally located to serve each of four 200-agent call center units. A new exterior of metal fascia and windows and an inviting interior of warm colors, ergonomic furnishings and selections from the company's antique poster collection apply the finishing touches for a Cinderella-style happy ending.

Top left: Lunch room.

Top right: Call center operations.

Middle right: Call center operations desk.

Bottom right: Lounge.

Opposite: View through portal.

Photography: Mark Henninger, Imagic Digital.

NELSON

Corporate Effective Work Practices Program
Charlotte, North Carolina

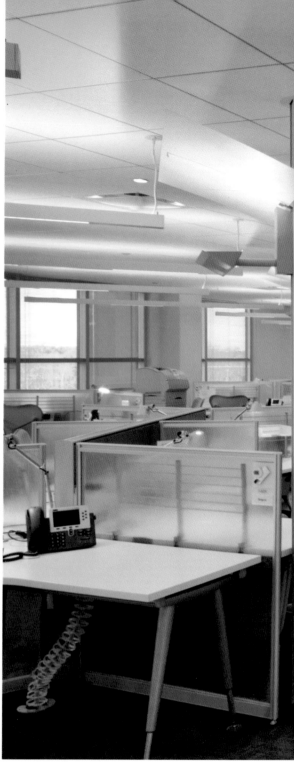

"The future is not what it used to be," as the French like to say. Momentous changes in the global economy are forcing businesses to develop innovative strategies, clarify core values, and learn new ways to measure their effectiveness. For a corporate client, the NELSON team recently designed an Effective Work Practices pilot program, installed in Charlotte, North Carolina, to reshape its real estate portfolio, "brand" the workplace, and position it as the "Employer of Choice." The project represents an ambitious take on what the modern office should be. Three main goals, creating a choice of where and when to work, attracting and retaining world-class employees, and enabling an effective response to growth with manageable capital expenditures, have been achieved through a dynamic, wireless design that maximizes space efficiency, provides a varied menu of work settings, and is decidedly contemporary in form and function. In its visibly differentiated areas, mobile and full-time associates are clearly delineated, yet the design is fully integrated to welcome everyone inside. The "On-Stage Area," for example, is the greeting point for visitors and concierge services, and is accompanied by two large conference rooms

Above: Open plan area.

Right: Reception.

Opposite: Meeting silo.

Photography: Mark Henninger, Imagic Digital.

and a variety of smaller ones that rotate around each other in a convergence of meeting spaces convenient for all work zones. Dedicated areas, including 60 eight-foot by eight-foot and six 150-square-foot small conference rooms that can be converted to offices, are located at the far ends of the footprint in quiet zones. The drop-in area, available by reservation, accommodates mobile workers who need space for two to four hours with concentrated workstation clusters that can be turned into larger, more enclosed spaces with minimal installation effort. The Associate Center, furnished with informal, soft seating,

a coffee bar, water wall and virtual fireplace, lets associates engage in informal interaction even as it integrates the various work zones. As for the facility's effectiveness, its space plan registers an efficiency of 119 square feet per associate based on a 2:1 space utilization factor, and its interior design palette consists of flexible, durable and environmentally friendly materials, building products and furnishings. More importantly, the Effective Work Practices program is giving the company a competitive edge that talented workers are quickly putting to good use.

Top: Lounge and cyber-café.
Above: Cyber-café.

OPX, P.L.L.C.

21 Dupont Circle, NW
Washington, DC 20036
202.822.9797
202.785.0443 (Fax)
www.OPXGLOBAL.com

OPX, P.L.L.C.

German Marshall Fund of the United States
Washington, DC

Top right: Third floor conference room.

Top left: "Forum" public space.

Above: CEO's office.

Right: Top floor private office suite.

Bottom right: Café.

Opposite: Board room.

Photography: Judy Davis/ Hoachlander/Davis Photography.

Founded in 1972 through a gift from Germany as a permanent memorial to Marshall Plan assistance, the German Marshall Fund of the United States (GMF) made history itself in January with the opening of a new, five-level, 20,000-square-foot Washington, D.C. headquarters, designed by OPX. At the dedication of the facility, created by joining and renovating a 1912 mansion and an adjacent row house in historic Dupont Circle, German Chancellor Angela Merkel pointed out that the beautifully restored mansion housed West Germany's initial liaison to the Marshall Plan administration. Later it served as the country's diplomatic mission and embassy to the United States from 1952 to 1964. Preservation is just one of the project's accomplishments in creating a new home for GMF, a non-partisan American public policy institution promoting greater cooperation and understanding between the United States and Europe. Collectively, the board room, forum, private offices, open work stations and café retain the character of the historic structure and interiors. It seamlessly integrates the interiors of both buildings, and explores differing floor levels and scale to create dynamic and complex spaces—all with the approval of a rigorous historic review board. As Dr. Merkel happily observed, the design's success in integrating old with new and small with large parallels the mission of the German Marshall Fund itself.

OPX, P.L.L.C.

WorldSpace Incorporated
Silver Spring, Maryland

Eight months to develop a new facility—from the inception of the design process to the opening day—is a major challenge for any organization and its project team. However, eight months to develop a new, two-floor, 50,000-square-foot headquarters and regional operations center in Silver Spring, Maryland for WorldSpace Incorporated, a digital satellite radio service primarily for the emerging markets of Africa and Asia, also confronted its design firm, OPX, with complex technological and organizational requirements. Among the features of the new facility are a satellite control center, 12 broadcast studios, board room, seven

conference rooms, private offices, open work stations, café and such special provisions as 16 air-cooling units backed by redundant generators and a UPS system for 24/7 operations. To help WorldSpace meet its tight schedule, OPX closely coordinated its activities with the rest of the consulting team, comprising MEP engineers, structural engineers, acoustical engineers, communications integrators, lighting consultants, studio millworkers, raised floor manufacturers and security specialists. Daylight and views from the open offices and public gathering spaces along the perimeter brighten the glass-fronted private offices and

studios in the interior. As a result, WorldSpace's new, airy and open environment has opened on time and without distracting any customers among the five billion people in 130 countries served by the company.

Top: Regional operations center.

Above middle: Informal lounge.

Above: View into open plan area.

Left: Board room and café.

Opposite: Entrance.

Photography: Judy Davis/Hoachlander/Davis Photography.

OPX, P.L.L.C.

Watson Wyatt Worldwide
Arlington, Virginia

Left: Elevator lobby.
Bottom left: Board room.
Bottom center: Café.
Bottom right: Corridor.
Right: Reception area.

Photography: Judy Davis/ Hoachlander/Davis Photography.

Watson Wyatt Worldwide is a leading provider of human capital and financial management consulting services, with over $1.1 billion in revenue and some 6,000 associates in 30 countries. They wanted its new, five-floor, 122,000-square foot headquarters, in Arlington, Virginia, to capture the essence of its core values and vision "to create financial value through people, and for people." The award-winning contemporary design by OPX fulfills this wish in two distinctly different ways. First, it offers a rich mixture of working environments for individual and collaborative effort, consisting of private offices, open-plan work stations, conference rooms, small teaming spaces, multi-purpose room and café. Then, it decisively "brands" the space with the firm's global identity through space planning, design features, palette of finishes, and logo-based imagery, which has been incorporated in stone and carpet patterns. While the facility is anchored by the conference center located adjacent to the reception area, clusters of private offices and open-plan work stations support the various practice groups throughout the floors. Watson Wyatt Worldwide is so pleased with its new headquarters that it has adopted elements of the OPX design as standards for all its U.S. offices.

OPX, P.L.L.C.

BAE Systems Inc.
Arlington, Virginia

Private offices on the perimeter with glass fronts encircle war rooms for teaming and collaborative work, open-plan work stations, a presentation and demonstration area, a multi-purpose room, secure SCIF spaces and a café in the new, modern, three-floor, 60,000-square-foot office, designed by OPX for BAE Systems Inc., in Arlington, Virginia. If the space seems to portray a company with world-class technology, over 90,000 skilled personnel in some 130 countries, a solid reputation for corporate responsibility, and such advanced products as defense and aerospace systems, military aircraft, surface ships and submarines, that's no accident to the U.S. subsidiary of U.K.-based BAE Systems Inc. The design makes excellent use of a tight budget while reflecting its vital relationship with the federal government. However, it also surrounds BAE Systems in a highly functional, dynamic, state-of-the-art environment with natural light, sweeping views of metropolitan Washington, D.C., and a monumental stair connecting two of the three floors, in keeping with an organization that continuously tests the boundaries of sea, land and sky.

Above: Staircase and war room.
Top right: Stair landing.
Upper right: Demo area.
Right: Café.
Lower right: Elevator lobby.
Photography: Judy Davis/ Hoachlander/Davis Photography.

OWP/P

111 West Washington Street
Suite 2100
Chicago, IL 60602-2714
312.332.9600
312.332.9601 (Fax)
www.owpp.com

3101 North Central Avenue
Suite 770
Phoenix, AZ 85012-2645
602.294.6500
602.294.6565 (Fax)

OWP/P

Metropolitan Capital Bank
Chicago, Illinois

Urban professionals in Chicago who want the private banking services typically reserved for the wealthiest customers will find a warm welcome in a most unusual setting: a 92-year-old landmark building in the Arts & Crafts style just steps from bustling North Michigan Avenue. The new, four-story, 6,500-square-foot home of Metropolitan Capital Bank, designed by OWP/P, has transformed former residential artists' studios into a "financial studio," skillfully preserving and restoring the building's historic details while installing modern private offices, conference rooms and private banking amenities. The design aims to create a sophisticated environment where clients feel comfortable discussing personal financial matters.

A major reason for the project's success has been the close cooperation among MetCap Bank, its landlord, the Commission on Chicago Landmarks and the National Register of Historic Places. All parties needed to approve the proposed work, and good communications among them was critical. Aside from dealing with such discoveries as the absence of plumbing lines to half of the building, there were changes made to accommodate the bank's functional needs while remaining sympathetic to the original design, including portal openings between the historic suites to support internal circulation. The installation of custom furnishings, including furniture, rugs, draperies and lighting fixtures, applied the finishing touches. Appraising the

results, MetCap CEO Michael Rose says, "They blend so well together—the best of history and high technology—that the space seems both ageless and timeless."

Top left: Banking Great Room.
Top right: Boardroom.
Middle right: Meeting room.
Bottom right: Private office.
Opposite: Reception.
Photography: Christopher Barrett/Hedrich Blessing.

OWP/P

Segall Bryant & Hamill Investment Counsel
Chicago, Illinois

Distressing as it may be to their founders, young, entrepreneurial businesses inevitably change as they mature into established, profitable organizations. For Segall Bryant & Hamill Investment Counsel, a Chicago-based independent investment management firm founded in 1994 and dedicated to building long-lasting relationships with clients through consistent and exceptional service, the issue of change surfaced early in planning its new, 21,000-square-foot office, designed by OWP/P. At the partners' request, the public space represented by the reception area and main conference room features a magnificent skyline view and provides separation from the private space occupied by employees. But how would the design reflect the history of the firm and support evolving technology requirements in a way that would resonate with senior partners and simultaneously appeal to junior partners and guests? The design bridges the concerns of all parties by creating a contemporary environment combining sedate olive, beige and pale yellow tones with paneled walls of dark, rich mahogany and burled cherry, subtle lighting, original works of art and handsome transitional furnishings. "It looks like we've arrived," reports Ralph M. Segall, CFA, CIC, managing director, "but it doesn't go over the top. OWP/P hit it right on."

Above: Reception.

Opposite: Boardroom.

Photography: Steve Hall/Hedrich Blessing.

OWP/P

Comcast Spotlight
Chicago, Illinois

Count on Comcast Spotlight, the advertising sales division of Comcast Cable, to know how to put on a show. Its award-winning new, 32,500-square-foot regional advertising sales office in Chicago, designed by OWP/P, consolidates several existing offices in one location to create a dynamic and irresistibly energetic environment, infused with technology, that shows clients what Comcast does in ways they are unlikely to forget. While the facility contains such conventional office elements as private offices, open work stations and conference rooms, it also houses a master control center, editing suites, teaming/breakout spaces and a "museum" of technology that it uses to good effect. The "show" begins for clients at the reception desk, shaped like the Comcast "C," where they are welcomed to a waiting space inundated by live TV imagery projected onto fabric screens. The tempo quickens when visitors are escorted from the reception area. The first space they encounter is the master control center. Instead of being relegated to back-

OWP/P

of-house space, the facility is proudly displayed as a show-case of people, monitors and non-stop activity to promote Comcast, the nation's largest provider of cable services, as a great communicator. Next, a museum-like gallery highlights the history of tele-vision, cable and Comcast, and the journey ends at the editing suites for advertising production. Though most Comcast Spotlight employees do not face a daily routine quite as dramatic, they work in an equally appeal-ing workplace of abundant daylight, open-plan work sta-tions with low-height panels, and comfortable, contempo-rary furnishings. Basic and simple as the construction may be, composed largely of glass, metal and drywall, the impact of the design on clients has been as upbeat as a rave review.

Top: Museum corridor and master control center.

Bottom left: Hallway.

Bottom right: Boardroom.

Partridge Architects Inc.

Bell Atlantic Tower
1717 Arch Street
Suite 4101
Philadelphia, PA 19103
215.567.3595
215.557.7984 (Fax)
www.partridgearch.com

Partridge Architects Inc.

Michael Salove Company
Philadelphia, Pennsylvania

Above: Elevator lobby and reception.

Top right: Conference room.

Above right: Corner office.

Right: Perimeter offices.

Opposite: Central lounge.

Photography: Jeffrey Totaro.

Chances are if you're shopping or dining at an upscale retail location in Pennsylvania, New Jersey or Delaware, you're benefiting from the services of Philadelphia-based Michael Salove Company, a leading retail real estate advisory & brokerage firm in the region since 1989. The firm, offering expertise in retail tenant representation, owner/developer representation, urban retail advisory services and investment sales, isn't afraid to analyze its own needs. In fact, its new, single-floor, 5,300-square foot office, designed by Partridge Architects, meets three bold program requirements:

1) no doors anywhere, 2) an open plan environment with a large, central lounge/meeting area, and 3) a "cool" space reflecting the firm's upscale retail clients. To bring daylight and vitality from the private offices and conference room along the perimeter to the reception and lounge/meeting area in the center, the design creatively employs a glass interior wall between the conference room and central space, translucent acrylic walls for private offices, subdued lighting, bright colors, and stylish, modern furnishings. This advisor follows its own advice—with spectacular results.

Partridge Architects Inc.

Infinity Broadcasting
WOGL, WPHT and 610/WIP
Bala Cynwyd, Pennsylvania

While Infinity Broadcasting operates one of America's largest major-market radio networks, it tailors its stations to suit local audiences. Consider its new broadcast facility in Bala Cynwyd, a Philadelphia suburb. Here, on two floors, a 28,000-square foot space, designed by Partridge Architects, are three distinctly different stations: WOGL, playing local oldies, WPHT, carrying nationally syndicated talk radio, and 610/WIP, featuring sports talk radio. Their facilities include such conventional components as a reception area, private offices, work stations, conference rooms, eight studios, two production rooms, three edit booths, technical operations center, lunchroom and restrooms. Yet there were interesting challenges to resolve.

To accommodate dissimilar functional groups—three radio stations, station support and sales—without compromising security or space, the design incorporates unobtrusive secured control points. To give the radio stations individual identities, each received its own palette of colors, materials and finishes. To meet exacting technical requirements for power, the technical operations center has raised access flooring, supplemental AC units, a UPS and a 100kw backup generator. Listeners may not notice the improvements, but Janet Kowalczyk, Infinity's market engineering manager, declares, "I love it. You guys really outdid yourselves on this one."

Top: WOGL/WPHT conference room.

Above: 610/WIP reception area.

Right: WOGL/WPHT TOC.

Opposite top: WOGL/WPHT lobby.

Opposite bottom left: 610/WIP studio.

Opposite bottom right: WOGL studio.

Photography: Jeffrey Totaro.

Partridge Architects Inc.

Wallace Roberts & Todd, LLC
Philadelphia, Pennsylvania

Clients of Wallace Roberts & Todd, LLC value the way this distinguished interdisciplinary planning and design practice solves their problems through innovative urban design that conserves and improves the natural and cultural characteristics of their regions.

Thus, when WRT needed a new, one-floor, 30,600-square foot office in downtown Philadelphia, Partridge Architects was asked to create an interior design as forward-looking as the firm's own work. The classic modern design solves three formidable problems. First, collaboration and cross-disciplinary communication are encouraged in two spatial environments, namely open "pin-up" areas adjacent to circulation paths and communal team meeting areas at all four corners of the main studio. While the "pin-up" areas facilitate casual encounters, the meeting areas occupy some of the most attractive spaces in the facility. Then, access to daylight and views is provided for the entire staff by locating private offices, conference rooms and support spaces in glass-walled enclosures surrounding the building core and west side of the building, where the firm's administrative and management personnel are located. Window positions, traditionally the prerogative of managers, become a universal amenity in this manner without denying the privacy of walls to those who require it. Finally, the construction reflects Wallace Roberts & Todd's legacy of commitment to ecological design through adherence to the green design requirements of the U.S. Green Building Council for LEED-CI certification. For example, recycled-content materials are used extensively, such as carpet tile containing 40 percent recycled content, and desktops made from

Above: Reception/lobby.

Opposite top: Elevator lobby.

Opposite bottom: Team meeting room.

Photography: Raber Photography.

Partridge Architects Inc.

Wallace Roberts & Todd, LLC
Philadelphia, Pennsylvania

renewable woodstalk board. In addition, regional manufacturers supplied over 40 percent of products and materials, and 75 percent of construction waste was recycled. Better yet, the space is as attractive as it is functional. Bright accent colors are used against a neutral environment of white walls, gray carpet, neutral finishes, and handsome modern furnishings. The sophisticated lighting employs a light shelf that bounces light from the corridor deep into the space, as well as light sensors and occupancy sensors to exploit daylight, conserve energy and control glare and heat

gain. Not only has the award-winning design drawn praise from Wallace Roberts & Todd, it has been accorded the prestigious LEED-CI Gold Certification.

Above: Corridor with light shelves.

Above right: View from lobby to conference room.

Right: Conference room.

Photography: Raber Photography.

184

Perkins+Will

330 N. Wabash Ave.
Suite 3600
Chicago, IL 60611
312.755.0770
312.755.0775 (Fax)
www.perkinswill.com

Perkins+Will

Digitas
Chicago, Illinois

Space never sits idly at the Chicago office of Digitas, an indirect marketing company that enables blue-chip global brands to develop profitable digital, direct and indirect relationships with their customers. In its new, one-floor, 28,000-square-foot facility for 140 employees, designed by Perkins+Will, Digitas makes intensive use of multi-functional and reconfigurable client presentation spaces that form the heart of this open and boldly modern environment, which also includes a reception area, open-plan offices, private offices, teaming spaces, café and gallery. What makes the design so effective is its careful yet imaginative use of floor area, budget and time. Private workspaces and group areas, for example, are tightly configured but equipped with amenities. Standard building materials are used in unique ways to achieve custom effects. Sheet vinyl makes an uncommon appearance in a corporate facility to help create its clean, modern look, along with cold cathode lighting in public areas and bright punches of color that spike an otherwise neutral color scheme. As a result, Digitas happily observes that the space is its brand, no small compliment coming from a world-class marketing organization.

Above: Reception.

Top right: View from conference room.

Right: Waiting area.

Bottom right: Hallway to open office area.

Opposite: Breakout.

Photography: Anthony May.

186

Perkins+Will

Bloomberg, L.P.
Chicago, Illinois

One of the reasons Bloomberg is a leading global provider of data, news and analytics could well be the offices it constructs for its work force, as typified by a new, 8,000-square-foot news bureau and sales office for 50 employees in Chicago, designed by Perkins+Will. A Bloomberg workplace is open, transparent, egalitarian and effective. Not only does the Chicago facility fully integrate its state-of-the-art presentation audio-visual systems with the interior architecture, but it also incorporates extensive multi-functionality, and making every square foot count in fulfilling an extensive program of activities, while establishing a cool, sophisticated modern environment that supports its occupants and extends the Bloomberg "brand." This multi-layered space is a study in contrasts, using glass extensively to create a reception area, open office space, television studio, training room, central pantry and fish tank, balancing the sleek, shimmering surfaces with stylish and custom modern furnishings. Happily, the contrast works. The design lets employees work comfortably and efficiently, and look good while doing so. In the bottom-line-driven world Bloomberg monitors for its audiences in 126 countries, that's a heck of a deal.

Below: View of Pantry.
Bottom: Training room.
Opposite top right: Touchdown area.
Opposite top left: Conference room.
Opposite bottom: Reception.
Photography: Chris Barrett/ Hedrich Blessing.

Perkins+Will

Allina Corporate Headquarters
Minneapolis, Minnesota

Above: Executive reception.
Right: Main lobby.
Bottom right: Open work space.
Bottom left: Knowledge center.
Opposite: Atrium.
Photography: Chris Barrett/ Hedrich Blessing.

To consolidate employees of Allina Hospitals & Clinics from 11 locations across metropolitan Minneapolis in one modern, efficient and flexible corporate headquarters, the not-for-profit network of hospitals, clinics and other health care services, active in Minnesota and western Wisconsin, recently developed a new home that simultaneously stands as a symbol of renewal. Allina has developed an airy, spacious and well-lighted 10-story, 418,000-square-foot headquarters for 1,800 employees, designed by Perkins+Will, within the walls of a former Sears retail store and warehouse originally built in 1929. The project is a model of historic renovation and re-use, refurbishing the brick-clad concrete structure while introducing an up-to-date work environment. Inevitably, numerous challenges emerged during the conversion. Since the existing deep floor plates excluded daylight from the interior, a 24-foot by 60-foot atrium was cut into all 10 floors that not only delivers natural light, but also helps unify the employees. Where low warehouse ceilings could have been lowered still more by mechanical, electrical and sprinkler systems, the designers and engineers devised innovative solutions that preserve height. The new office environment is almost entirely open, since the CEO wants only open-plan offices and no private offices, along with a reception area, executive suite, conference center, training center, knowledge center, cafeteria and huddle rooms. To foster greater collaboration, Allina's modern furnishings are juxtaposed with existing brick exterior walls and concrete columns and ceiling deck. In fact, the new interiors, featuring classic Eames seating and tables, look splendid within the 77-year-old building.

Perkins+Will

Dougherty Financial Group
Minneapolis, Minnesota

Design becomes a strategic business tool when organizations know how to use it. Consider the new, two-floor, 35,000-square-foot office of Dougherty Financial Group in downtown Minneapolis, designed by Perkins+Will. The national money management, trading and investment banking firm, a repeat client of Perkins+Will for three decades, wanted to rethink its space, following the sale of some divisions, to provide a cohesive look for the firm's clients as well as 160 employees. A sophisticated yet welcoming residential feeling greets visitors once they enter the reception area and its bronze-leafed dome. The balance of the new environment, a traditional layout with board room and conference suite adjacent to reception, private offices on the perimeter, open work stations, training rooms and lunchroom in the interior, and a 55-position trading operation on its own floor, continue the mood with neutral colors, Wenge flooring, fabric wallcoverings, bronze, limestone, leather and mohair fabrics, and residential-style furnishings. To complete the traditional image, the design makes inspired use of daylight, aided by clerestory windows, spectacular views of the Minneapolis skyline, particularly in the board room, and the glow of strategically placed spotlights, showcasing Dougherty's world-class art collection.

Top left: Boardroom.
Above: Corridor.
Left: Lobby.
Photography: Dana Wheelock.

192

Roger Ferris + Partners

285 Riverside Avenue
Westport, CT 06880
203.222.4848
203.222.4856 (Fax)
www.ferrisarch.com

Roger Ferris + Partners

FactSet Research Systems Inc.
Norwalk, Connecticut

The financial world has counted on FactSet Research Systems Inc., a major supplier of global financial and economic information, for fundamental data on tens of thousands of companies worldwide since 1978. FactSet, which combines over 200 data bases into its dedicated online service, along with the tools needed to download, combine and manipulate the data for investment analysis, clearly values order, efficiency and accuracy in its work. To achieve a better fit between the design of its Norwalk, Connecticut headquarters and its daily, on-site activities, the company recently asked Roger Ferris + Partners to design an 8,760-square-foot addition and renovation. This has streamlined the entry sequence into its lobby and remodeled the cafeteria for proper circulation flow and greater exposure to natural light and outdoor views. The successful outcome, including an appropriately elegant entrance lobby and reception area, focused on an outdoor courtyard, a dramatic cafeteria with sunny and spacious dining rooms, and open office spaces with crisply detailed private offices and conference rooms enclosed in glass, has made FactSet's headquarters the equal of its products and services.

Top: Cafeteria.
Above left: Private offices.
Above right: Conference room.
Right: Waiting area.
Opposite: Reception.
Photography: ©Paúl Rivera/ archphoto.

Roger Ferris + Partners

RK Restaurant
Rye, New York

Can you name a restaurant you'd revisit at the drop of a dime—your dime, that is? M.H. Reed, a restaurant critic for the *New York Times*, recently identified establishments in metropolitan New York that reviewers would consider patronizing on their own, and included RK, a 144-seat, 5,241-square-foot space in Rye, New York for its "TriBeCa chic" that "defies its suburban location." RK's

appeal isn't hard to fathom. When the proprietors of the popular eatery Rebecca's in nearby Greenwich, Connecticut, chef Reza Khorshidi and his wife Rebecca Kirhoffer, were ready to expand their business, they asked their architect, Roger Ferris + Partners, to transform an abandoned Rye warehouse into a thoroughly modern RK for fusion cuisine. To do this, the architect has made the

exterior resemble the original structure, and filled it with a ravishing white minimal interior of three dining rooms on three levels. They offset their minimal decoration with such dramatic elements as a sensuous, back-lighted bar, a kitchen enshrined in a glass pavilion, shimmering, floor-to-ceiling window walls, and a sophisticated lighting design supplemented by a light installation that projects

provocative phrases ("I think she's cheating but I don't blame her") on the wall. Better make your reservation now.

That kitchen gleams, it looks like

Above: Dining room facing kitchen.

Left: Kitchen.

Opposite top: Evening exterior view.

Opposite left: Dinning room detaila.

Opposite right: Bar.

Photography: ©Paúl Rivera/ archphoto.

Roger Ferris + Partners

Morgan Stanley
Harrison, New York

Acquiring Texaco's four-story, 750,000-square-foot former headquarters, in Harrison, New York, has been part of an overall effort by Morgan Stanley to meet its space needs and business continuity planning requirements in the wake of September 11. (This leading investment bank, the largest tenant at the World Trade Center, lost nearly 1.2 million square feet of office space in the terrorist attack.) To prepare a vast structure that has been portrayed as "a skyscraper lying on its side" for its new mission, Morgan Stanley asked Roger Ferris + Partners to create a design that would upgrade the entire space, bring its infrastructure up to date, and insert a trading floor in what was previously an outdoor courtyard. "No corner was left unturned" as the architect proceeded to address the issues imposed by building technology, structural integrity, acoustics, lighting and climate control. The result is a classic modern office building with state-of-the-art building systems and interiors custom tailored to Morgan Stanley's requirements. For example, the remodeled dining facility, which features new finishes and lighting, a modernized servery and a new coffee bar beside a new glass stair that leads to the lobby, can now double as an assembly space for up to 350 people. The lobby itself sports a new entry sequence with a new portal that marks the entry on the front façade, and uses a new reception desk and seating area to round out the sequence. A new, 15-room corporate conference center has been integrated with the building, incorporating the existing auditorium as its heart. Perhaps the most difficult challenge,

Top left: Reception.
Top right: Skylight.
Above: View towards servery.

Opposite: Staircase.
Photography: ©Paúl Rivera/ archphoto.

Roger Ferris + Partners

Morgan Stanley
Harrison, New York

converting the eastern-most outdoor courtyard into a trading floor for 1,200 traders, demonstrates what can be accomplished by a diligent consultant team and an attentive client. While conceptual layouts of the trading floor and its enclosure were initiated as soon as programming information was received from various business units, the entire project team looked to Morgan Stanley's executive committee for commentary and advice. The best corporate facilities are designed as instruments of corporate strategy, and Morgan Stanley demonstrates just how effective a good workplace environment can be.

Above: Cafeteria main dining area.
Left: Fitness center.

RTKL Associates Inc.

1250 Connecticut Avenue
4th Floor
Washington, DC 20036
202.833.4400
202.887.5168 (Fax)
www.rtkl.com

RTKL Associates Inc.

Chiao Tung Bank
Taipei, Taiwan

Right: Display case.
Below: Branch bank.
Bottom: Financial services.
Opposite: Teller desk.
Photography: David Whitcomb.

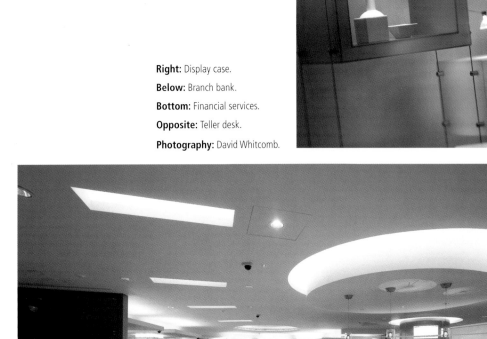

Entrepreneurs in Taiwan know where to turn for such financial services as equity funding, venture capital investment, and mid- to long-term development credit: Chiao Tung Bank. A major subsidiary of Mega Financial Holding Co., Chiao Tung is Taiwan's largest development bank with $16 billion in assets. Having previously operated as an industrial bank, it recently reinvented its public image with the help of RTKL, which successfully re-branded Tokyo's Shinsei Bank. To create a banking environment reflecting the bank's identity and client values, the design combines the high technology of user-friendly ATMS in sleek metallic structures and flat-screen computers with such warm touches as recessed lighting, cool colors, curving, organic architectural forms, and comfortable leather seating. The streamlined style, seen in a Taipei branch bank that will serve as a model for future remodeling and expansion, is simultaneously functional, sophisticated and relaxed. Not bad qualities for today's bank—or banker, either.

RTKL Associates Inc.

Oceaneering Advanced Technologies Group
Hanover, Maryland

How do you turn a 93,650-square foot warehouse in Hanover, Maryland into a two-story, 51,240-square foot office and one-story, 93,650-square foot technical component for an advanced applied technology company seeking to make a big impression and strong branding statement on a low budget? RTKL has designed a functional yet dramatic new facility for Oceaneering Advanced Technologies Group, a provider of engineered services and hardware to oil and gas companies, government agencies and firms in aerospace, marine engineering and construction industries operating in marine, space, and other harsh environments. Its solution: Use low-cost materials in creative ways, concentrating on public areas. The front-of-house area projects a nautical spirit through such memorable elements as a canted, two-story wall resembling a ship's hull, while the back-of-house area is handled economically using accent paints, minimal perimeter offices and a large, open central space to enliven the open-plan landscape, launching Oceaneering in style.

Top right: Curving corridor.
Top left: Entrance to conference room.
Left: Staircase.
Opposite: Reception.
Photography: Erik Kvalsvik.

RTKL Associates Inc.

Sub-Zero/Wolf/KWC Showrooms
Charlotte, North Carolina and Atlanta, Georgia

The home kitchen has not been the same since Westye F. Bakke founded the Sub-Zero Freezer Company in a Madison, Wisconsin garage in 1945. Having acquired the Wolf Appliance Company in 2000, the company now displays its high-end refrigerators alongside Wolf's professional-grade ranges by promoting a modern lifestyle centered on the kitchen. It's a potent vision that RTKL celebrates with award-winning designs in a 6,000-square foot historic renovation in Charlotte and a 14,000-square foot new space in Atlanta. Each showroom, comprising conference rooms, dining areas, reception and training rooms, offers interactive kitchens, active plumbing displays and a private wine cellar for live demonstrations by professional chefs. The showrooms' power comes from presenting appliances as works of art, surrounded by the design motifs of prestigious, contemporary homes, lighted, detailed and furnished to perfection. As a company spokesperson says, "Your excellent design skills helped make our new Charlotte showroom a piece of art."

Top: Demonstration kitchen.
Above left: Reception.
Above: Bathroom.
Left: Dining area.
Opposite: Kitchen vignette.
Photography: Jeffrey Jacobs.

RTKL Associates Inc.

Credit Suisse Private Advisors
Miami, Florida

Diamonds are small but precious, and the new, 3,000-square foot Miami office for Credit Suisse Private Advisors, designed by RTKL, clearly understands that. The overall dimensions of the reception area, conference room, private offices, employee lounge and storage facility in a high-end financial facility are relatively modest. The design transcends its limits to establish the luxurious and residential ambience expected by the affluent private banking clientele of Credit Suisse Private Advisors, a Zurich-based company providing investment counseling to highly qualified individuals and families domiciled in the United States and to the people and institutions that advise them. The design team brilliantly exploits the ability of an innovative storefront system to partition the gallery-like space without beeing confining. The design and draws on quartz flooring, custom wall finishes, fine, contemporary furnishings and collected pieces, and subtle lighting to complete the ideal setting to contemplate maximizing returns and minimizing risks.

Top: Reception/waiting area.
Far right: Conference room.
Right: Employee lounge.
Photography: Grossman Photography.

Spillis Candela DMJM

800 Douglas Entrance
North Tower 2nd Floor
Coral Gables, FL 33134
305.444.4691
305.447.3580 (Fax)
www.spilliscandeladmjm.com

Above: Coffee shop in lobby view.

Right: Private office.

Opposite: Corridor.

Photography: Nick Merrick/ Hedrich Blessing.

Business leaders who have yet to harness the power of design to help foster professional creativity and promote communication can learn much from the interior architecture of this newly renovated Corporate Headquarters. Since the project involved a registered historical building, the Corporation and its architect, Spillis Candela DMJM, worked with state authorities as well as the National Register for Historic Places to strike a good balance between old and new. However, the 250,000-square-foot building starts with a timeless premise by engaging the outdoors with a central exterior courtyard, which has terraces flanking the perimeter. Informal communication is fostered through common building amenities and situational opportunities that have been incorporated in the design.

The lower terrace level, for example, has been conceived like a retail and hospitality setting, and includes a cafeteria, conference/training center, fitness center, travel agency, hair salon, company store, copy center, clinic and self-storage center. Their individual spaces, positioned along the high traffic, high visibility finished "mall" corridor, are fitted out much as retail tenants would expect. Yet there are also creative details visible on the two typical upper floors, the partial penthouse floor and the full terrace/basement level that is partially below grade under the central courtyard. The penthouse floor is dedicated to flexible creative space for problem solving task forces and presentation. All walls in this area are suitable for writing, including operable partitions that serve to define teaming areas within the open space. Food service and an outdoor terrace add to the effectiveness of this think tank facility. The project also includes a detached auditorium, executive area with boardroom and conference rooms, office areas and three distinctive food service venues, including a coffee/sandwich bar, formal dining and corporate cafeteria. The existing executive offices open onto the exterior terrace balconies, which overlook a park-like setting. Adding to the uniqueness of the facility are many custom-designed building elements using aluminum. Clearly, this is a Corporate Headquarters where creativity and communication will flourish.

Spillis Candela DMJM

BankAtlantic Corporate Center
Fort Lauderdale, Florida

One of the largest financial institutions headquartered in Florida, 79-branch BankAtlantic wants customers and employees to regard it as a warm, convenient and accessible community bank. Consider the new, two-floor, 180,000-square-foot BankAtlantic Corporate Center in Fort Lauderdale, designed by Spillis Candela DMJM. The project has turned an old warehouse that had undergone major demolition of its interior spaces and tentative alteration of its front façade into a lively and prominent headquarters. Its award-winning design teaches how color, texture, pattern, lighting and planning can yield results that are visually imposing and cost-effective. For instance, strategic application of the corporate colors, red and blue, delivers a playful jolt to an otherwise calming color palette, exploiting contrasts in color and texture to emphasize BankAtlantic's "big family" image. Linear carpet installed perpendicular to corridor widths and large squares of accent color carpet help break up lengthy corridors. Vinyl and linoleum flooring, banquettes and café chairs and tables bring aesthetics and durability to the cafeteria space, located in the building's center under a large, circular skylight, so it can function as a meeting facility and social gathering place. Throughout this ambitious facility, housing a reception area, conference center, executive offices, open offices, copy center, cafeteria, fitness center, new mom lounge, check processing area and warehouse space,

BankAtlantic employees seem to be having a good time conducting business.

Top left: Typical corridor.
Above: Main reception.
Right: Corridor with skylight.
Opposite: Cafeteria.
Photography: Mike Butler.

Spillis Candela DMJM

American Airlines Admirals Club
JFK International Airport
New York, New York

Being an American Airlines "Admiral" was a rare honor in 1939, when chairman C.R. Smith welcomed VIP passengers and friends of the airline to the Admirals Club, a special place to relax before or after a flight at New York's LaGuardia Airport. Membership became open to all in 1967, and there are now close to 50 Admirals Clubs in the Americas, Europe and Asia. One of the newest examples, the one-story, 11,300-square-foot lounge in New York's JFK International Airport, designed by Spillis Candela DMJM, illustrates why travelers appreciate them as distinctive oases of peace imparting the flavor of their locales. The facility houses a check-in reception area, cyber–café, work stations, business center, children's room, TV lounges, quiet area, bar, coffee bar, food service, kitchen and shower. To give it a club-like ambiance with the spirit of New York, the design combines stone, wood, colored and frosted glass, modular carpet and stylish yet comfortable furnishings with vintage black-and-white photography depicting everything from construction workers atop the city's iconic skyscrapers to historic baseball games played at Yankee Stadium, Ebbets Field and the Polo Grounds. Visiting "Admirals" will also find numerous other delightful details, such as replicas of manhole covers in the shower area flooring, to remind them the Big Apple is just a cab, bus or subway ride away.

Top left: TV lounge.
Top right: Bar lounge.
Left: Reception.
Photography: Mike Butler.

216

Staffelbach Design Associates

2525 Carlisle
Dallas, TX 75201
214.452.1283
214.224.3075 (Fax)
www.staffelbach.com

Staffelbach Design Associates

Smith Group Asset Management
Dallas, Texas

Being totally focused on its clients' business and how to gain a competitive edge in its work has reaped rewards for Smith Group Asset Management, a Dallas-based registered investment advisor that provides equity investment management services for foundations, endowments, corporate pensions, public funds, multi-employer plans and high net worth individuals. Since its founding in 1978 by CEO Stephen S. Smith, CFA, Smith Group has specialized in finding attractively valued companies that will report a succession of positive earnings surprises. Its ability to predict positive earnings surprises—above 85 percent during the average quarter—is reflected in the new, one-story, 7,500-square-foot office, designed by Staffelbach Design

Associates. This timeless, contemporary space of stone, wood, carpet and drywall is designed to support the collegial atmosphere that thrives among its employees. It provides them such key facilities as the reception area, private offices, conference rooms, trading area and break room, all arranged with full visibility of operations from any vantage point. Comments Blake Estess, managing director of Smith Group, "Our space creates a wonderful impression of who we are."

Above: Reception.
Above left: Private offices.
Right: Trading area.
Opposite: Conference center.
Photography: Joseph Aker/ Aker/Zvonkovic Photography.

Staffelbach Design Associates

Hunt Petroleum Corporation
Dallas, Texas

Right: Connecting stair.
Below: Elevator lobby.
Opposite: Reception area.
Photography: Joseph Aker/
Aker/Zvonkovic Photography

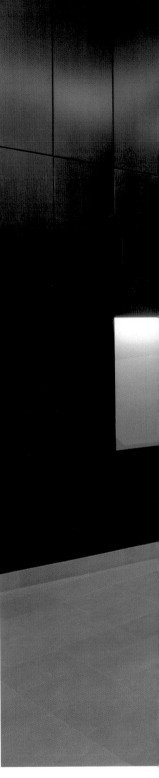

Engineers are clearly the focus of a new, two-story, 27,618-square-foot Dallas office for 80 employees of Hunt Petroleum Corporation, designed by Staffelbach Design Associates. Paying close attention to the layout of their drafting tables, map display spaces and storage units, as well as an unusually large amount of high-density filing, is nothing new for a conservative oil exploration and production company that conducts operations principally in Texas, Louisiana, Mississippi, North Dakota, the Gulf of Mexico, and the Dutch sector of the North Sea. Yet the overall design, encompassing a two-story reception area, private offices, open offices, conference rooms and employee dining in addition to high-density file rooms, attends to the needs of other employees as well. Informal meeting areas at the corners of both floors, for example, encourage communication among employees, while clear circulation paths let daylight penetrate all interior spaces. A dignified corporate

environment of cherry wood, limestone, stainless steel with brass accents, carpet, fabric and vinyl wallcoverings, sophisticated lighting and fine transitional furnishings pleases everyone. In praising the facility, Theresa Woods, vice president, human resources for Hunt observes, "The positive paradigm of Hunt Petroleum's culture have been further nurtured and reinforced by the design created by Staffelbach."

Staffelbach Design Associates

Brazos Private Equity Partners
Dallas, Texas

Left: Reception view into room foyer.

Bottom: Reception/lobby.

Opposite: Partner office.

Photography: Joseph Aker/ Aker/Zvonkovic Photography.

The partners of Brazos Private Equity Partners have extensive relationships that prove invaluable in generating investment opportunities and enhancing the value of portfolio investments. So it's not unusual that the firm's new, one-story, 7,500-square foot Dallas office for 10 employees, designed by Staffelbach Design Associates, strikes a tactful balance between an effective working environment to support high level financial transactions and numerous, individualized settings that address the partners' personal desires. The image of the new facility is a unified one, nevertheless, presenting a meticulously detailed transitional space of stone, wood, carpet, fabric and fine furnishings that seems to fit the firm like a bespoke tailored suit. For Brazos, a private invest-

Staffelbach Design Associates

Below: Board room.
Bottom right: Partner office.
Bottom left: Kitchen view from board room.

ment firm that specializes in leveraged acquisitions and recapitalizations of middle-market companies offering the potential for substantial capital appreciation for such investors as financial institutions, endowments, pension funds, plus highly successful CEOs and entrepreneurs, this is the fourth office relocation planned and designed by Staffelbach Design Associates. Evidently, the firm's long-term perspective towards its clients and investments extends to its design firm, which it has warmly praised for the design of its latest home.

224

Ted Moudis Associates

79 Madison Avenue
New York, NY 10016
212.308.4000
212.561.2020 (Fax)
www.tedmoudis.com

One Financial Place
440 South LaSalle Street
Chicago, IL 60605
312.663.0130
312.663.0138 (Fax)

Ted Moudis Associates

Metrovest Equities
New York, New York

Metrovest Equities, a real estate investment and development company, was looking for an installation that would reflect their dynamic work ethic and that would also serve as a tranquil foundation. They found their home in a classically modern, 15,000 square foot space located on the top commercial floor of a new state-of-the-art office building in the heart of midtown Manhattan. The design by Ted Moudis Associates emulates elegant simplicity. The reverse L-shaped floor plan comprises of a reception area, boardroom, executive suite, open area and a few private offices. An undulating drywall ceiling visually leads you from the reception through the boardroom, which has breathtaking views. The magnificent view envelops the entire perimeter of the space. Full-height glass panels and sliding door glass partitions were brought in to define the executive suite, administrative area and the private offices without visual boundaries. Breaking away from the linear office plan, a "triple egg" structure that comprises of a pantry, lounge and "think pod" was centrally located to encourage interaction. The use of natural and refined materials such as: French walnut, nickel mesh, composite stone, and clear glass allow the space to pay homage to the company's roots in construction.

Above: Executive suite.

Right: Reception waiting and boardroom.

Opposite bottom right: "Triple egg" pantry and lounge.

Opposite bottom left: Executive lounge.

Photography: Peter Paige.

Ted Moudis Associates

Knight Capital Group, Inc.
Jersey City, New Jersey

Knight Capital Group is a leading financial services firm that provides comprehensive trade execution solutions and asset management services. The company wanted an open and transparent design for their new, four level, 150,000 square foot headquarters in Jersey City. The offices, which include a trading floor, executive suite, conferencing center, open operational areas, data center and fitness center, are a tangible symbol for the growth and transition the company has made over the last few years. Ted Moudis Associates' design exudes elegance and sophistication and also encourages communication and flow. A connecting stairway, from the reception area to the trading floor, uses a clear glass balustrade that runs along a travertine stone wall, creating the illusion of an elegant floating structure. A gracious reception area with a glass balcony and an executive suite with private offices are positioned with unobstructed views of the double-height tiered trading floor. Simultaneously, the materials and furnishings that fit out the room, as well as the rest of the facility, include figured woods, polished marble, bronze metal and classic furniture that temper a modern function with refined tradition.

Right: Trading room.

Below: Conference room.

Bottom left: Reception.

Opposite top left: Board room.

Opposite top right: Executive suite.

Opposite bottom: Elevator lobby.

Photography: Peter Paige.

228

Ted Moudis Associates

Ospraie Management, LLC
New York, New York

Ospraie Management, a growing asset firm, wanted an open, welcoming environment balanced with a level of security appropriate for their business functions. They found their new headquarters in a 15,000 square foot office in a prime Park Avenue location. Ted Moudis Associates demonstrates an intelligently designed elegant space comprising of private offices, open areas, conference rooms and a trading area. Architectural elements, with a classically modern design, not only define the space but also act as a "roadmap" to help navigate around the core and also highlight key functional elements throughout the space. The reception area is located completely within the elevator lobby allowing the rest of the floor to be used entirely for private and open office areas. At night the core office is secured by a sliding glass door. A glowing onyx wall provides a dramatic backdrop to the dark brown, wenge wood reception desk which also acts as a secure home for the technology that supports the receptionist. Upon leaving the reception area, there is a ropery cherry wall that acts as a space divider and as a storage closet with multiple file drawers. Another onyx feature, lit primarily by daylight, acts as the front wall of one of the client conference rooms and provides a focal point that draws one towards the boardroom. Along this corridor is a volume of ice-blue glass

that is the trading room. The board room entrance is then located between the blue-glass of the trading room and the onyx wall of the conference rooms. If form follows function in modern design, this design demonstrates that function can return the compliment.

Below: Open-plan work stations and private offices.

Bottom left: Meeting room.

Bottom right: Corridor and trading room.

Opposite: Elevator lobby/reception.

Photography: Peter Paige.

Ted Moudis Associates

MatlinPatterson Global Advisors
New York, New York

MatlinPatterson, a private equity firm focused on control distressed investing, was looking for an office space that conveyed their seriousness and integrity all while defining them within their industry. There was a preference for strong site lines that created an environment free of hierarchy. Ted Moudis Associates generated a 20,000 square foot office that incorporated a guest lounge, two large boardrooms, open plan workstations, perimeter private offices and a large residential kitchen. MatlinPatterson's objectives were accomplished through careful selection of under-stated materials, furnishing and finishes such as woven carpets, marble, lacquered walnut paneling, mohair and leather. Elegant and simple details, utilizing classic materials like lacquered wood and polished marbles were also used throughout. In order to maintain seamless interaction between all divisions of the company, an open layout, from north to south, was created to maximize site lines. A large kitchen and lounge spaces were incorporated to foster communication. The implementation of details, such as video conferencing and electrified glazing, in combination with residential touches such as draperies, pendant fixtures and lounge areas were created in order to utilize the current infrastructure and technology.

VOA Associates Incorporated

224 S. Michigan Avenue
Suite 1400
Chicago, IL 60604
312.554.1400
312.554.1412 (Fax)
www.voa.com

VOA Associates Incorporated

Julien J. Studley Inc.
Chicago, Illinois

You will sense its presence in every office developed by Studley, a leading commercial real estate services firm specializing in tenant representation, since it was founded by Julien J. Studley in 1954. A genuine respect for modern architecture reflects the founder's enthusiasm for Le Corbusier and other modern masters. Half a century later, Studley's new, one-floor, 15,291-square-foot Chicago office for 55 employees, designed by VOA Associates, has met the firm's request for a clean, International Style image with an award-winning tribute to that vigorous period in the history of architecture. The largely open facility, which includes reception, private offices, inboard work stations, conference rooms and lunchroom, happens to be an excellent workplace, offering generous spaces and natural light to all employees directly through perimeter windows or indirectly through glazed fronts for private offices and even a translucent blue window separating the main conference room from reception. But the powerful design motifs, such as the interlocking L-shapes that appear in ceiling soffits, walls, work stations and carpet patterns, the striking color scheme employing primary accent colors, and the concealed, built-in lighting, are the reasons this environment intrigues staff and visitors alike.

Above: Reception area.

Right: North view with reception and boardroom.

Below: Break room.

Opposite bottom left: Secretarial work stations.

Opposite bottom right: Boardroom.

Photography: Nick Merrick/ Hedrich Blessing.

VOA Associates Incorporated

RR Donnelley
Chicago, Illinois

When you have witnessed the significant changes in technology and business experienced by RR Donnelley, the world's premier full-service provider of print and related services, including document-based business process outsourcing, how radical could an office relocation be? For 350 Chicago employees, moving from small, dense floor plates to new, open, organic and daylight-flooded spaces, designed by VOA Associates on four floors totaling 108,000 square feet, the change has been profound indeed. Steeped in history as the 142-year-old company undoubtedly is, it has evolved into a dynamic, forward-looking organization with 50,000 employees in some 600 locations across the globe. In Chicago, a 24/7 headquarters forms the heart of a new, post-merger/acquisition home that includes private offices, general office areas, library, pantry and other community spaces, and support facilities as well. The design emphasis here is on central community and public spaces with a 360-degree daylight penetration to encourage staff interaction. The new, modern setting should help keep RR Donnelley where it wants to be in the world of print and related services— right on top.

Top: Corridor.

Above left: Elevator entry and printed works display eabinets.

Above right: Glass front office and open-plan work stations.

Opposite: Main reception and entry to executive suite.

Photography: Christopher Barrett/Hedrich Blessing.

VOA Associates Incorporated

The LaSalle Bank Chicago Marathon
Chicago, Illinois

Above: Corridor with view to reception.

Left: Feature wall and work stations.

Opposite: View from board room to small meeting area.

Photography: Nick Merrick/ Hedrich Blessing.

Now entering its 29th year as a Chicago institution with a maximum of 40,000 runners who raise millions of dollars for charities, The LaSalle Bank Chicago Marathon has an exciting new, one-floor, 10,400-square-foot office, designed by VOA Associates, to keep pace with the event itself. The rectilinear space, which includes private offices, open work stations, meeting spaces, production-workroom space, lunch room, shower, massage room, lounge and storage space, contains the abundance of columns in the old building housing it with sinuous curves and undulating paths that encourage staff and visitors to move through it freely. Its spatial scheme represents the Windy City in a straightforward, symbolic way. One side portrays the city by featuring private offices and open work stations in tones of gray, the other side depicts support spaces as the parks and lakes using bright, high-energy colors. The circulation between the two halves is treated as the path of the marathon, enlivened by LEDs built into the curved walls that change colors. Lighting plays a conspicuous role throughout the office space

VOA Associates Incorporated

culminating in the conference room, where a dual-control cold cathode installation is outfitted for three different CRI and lamp color temperatures to complement the marketing media being presented in the room. Likewise, furnishings figure importantly in the design, since the classic modern pieces chosen by VOA Associates recall the vital role played by Chicago in the birth of modern architecture and design. Thus, the Marathon work force of 20 employees, who increase in number when the organization staffs up for specific events, can savor the sensation of being in constant motion even in an office six floors above the action.

Top left: Executive reception.
Far left: Corridor.
Left: Executive office.

Wolcott Architecture • Interiors

3859 Cardiff Avenue
Culver City, CA 90232
310.204.2290
310.838.6109 (Fax)
www.wolcottai.com

Wolcott Architecture • Interiors

THQ
Agoura Hills, California

Above: Game demo area.
Left: Break out area.
Opposite: Reception.
Photography: Marshal Safron.

When did you last play Company of Heroes, Destroy All Humans!, Juiced or Titan Quest? THQ, a worldwide developer and publisher of interactive entertainment software, founded in 1989, makes something for everyone. Enthusiastic games make the company a leader in the field, selling products throughout North America, Europe and Asia Pacific. Making order out of

the large footprint needed to house 400 employees at THQ's headquarters in Agoura Hills, California, has been another matter. The company's two-story, 100,000-square-foot space, combining private offices, open-plan work stations, conference rooms and lunch room, designed by Wolcott Architecture • Interiors, establishes a strong sense of place through good wayfinding, quality lighting and efficient yet interesting space utilization. The cost-effective design solution features an open/closed ceiling with indirect and direct lighting as well as added windows and skylights, a high-density layout for open-plan work stations that is angled for interest and offset by ample aisles and breakout areas. Although THQ takes itself seriously as a business, bright accent colors, varied lighting and contemporary furnishings that are both corporate and fun keep employees in touch with the games customers play.

Wolcott Architecture • Interiors

Korn/Ferry International
Los Angeles, California

A classic contemporary environment may be all a renowned organization needs to do business. That's just what Korn/Ferry International has achieved in its new, two-story, 36,000-square-foot corporate headquarters for 145 employees in Los Angeles, designed by Wolcott Architecture • Interiors. Korn/Ferry has been a leading executive recruitment firm for 37 years, serving the corporate world with services ranging from corporate governance and CEO recruitment to executive search, middle-management recruitment and Leadership Development Solutions, a suite of services including strategic management assessment, executive coaching and development, and supporting IT platforms. Floor plans for Korn/Ferry reflect a traditional scheme of private window offices and open administrative work stations that are appointed in such timeless materials as wood, limestone, glass and stainless steel with understated contemporary furnishings, sophisticated lighting and a connecting stair. But there's room for drama even in the most basic interior, and the opportunity comes as

soon as visitors arrive. Since Korn/Ferry wanted as much exterior view as possible in the reception area, the design shifts the conference room to an interior position with a glass façade to open up 70 linear feet of windows with panoramic views of Los Angeles that are unabashedly spectacular.

Wolcott Architecture • Interiors

Wilmington Trust
Orange County, California

Wilmington Trust is one of the nation's most respected independent financial services organizations. The company is known for the high quality of its people and services, which has made it a major player in personal trusts, wealth management and consumer and commercial banking services with clients in all 50 states and 59 foreign countries on six continents. For a business that began serving clients in 1901, Wilmington Trust remains refreshingly open to new thinking and innovations.

So when it asked Wolcott Architecture • Interiors to design a new, one-floor, 6,500-square-foot Orange County, California office, it encouraged the design team to develop a more open and better functioning environment for its 20 employees. The new workplace is primarily open as a result, featuring natural light that is visible everywhere, sophisticated indirect lighting that maximizes the effectiveness of reflective surfaces, open-plan work stations configured to encourage collaboration

without ignoring acoustic privacy, and minimal private offices behind glass for those who continue to need them, along with a reception area, conference facilities and lunchroom. The interior appointments, by contrast, combine enduring materials like wood, stone and glass with neutral colors and fine contemporary furnishings, reminding staff and visitors alike that innovation and tradition can work well together.

Above: Conference room.

Right: Reception area.

Opposite bottom right: Work station.

Opposite bottom left: Corridor.

Photography: Marshal Safron.

246

Wolcott Architecture • Interiors

Wolcott Architecture • Interiors
Culver City, California

Left: Wolcott reception.
Bottom left: Stair and mezzanine/staff area.
Photography: Marshal Safron.

An architecture firm that has designed over 25 million square feet of commercial and institutional space since its founding in 1975, serving clients in such far-ranging fields as aerospace, insurance, education, manufacturing, law and health care, could be expected to have grown significantly in personnel and operations.

For Wolcott Architecture • Interiors, a recent, 10,000-square-foot renovation and addition to its office in Culver City, California, represents just the latest milestone in more than 30 years of successful practice as a team-oriented organization. The addition not only improves the existing work environment to retain and attract employees, it deliberately integrates the new construction with the existing building, a high, open volume space originally constructed in the 1950s and enlarged in 1995. The combined structures appear to have been designed and completed at one time. The new and remodeled facilities, which include private offices, staff areas, library and conference room, place 50 employees in a calm, spacious and well lighted contemporary setting that will surely help them in designing the next 25 million square feet of space for Wolcott's clients.

Zimmer Gunsul Frasca Partnership

320 SW Oak Street
Suite 500
Portland, OR 97204
503.224.3860
503.224.2483 (Fax)
www.zgf.com

925 Fourth Avenue
Suite 2400
Seattle, WA 98104
206.623.9414
206.623.7868 (Fax)

515 South Flower Street
Suite 3700
Los Angeles, CA 90071
213.617.1901
213.617.0047 (Fax)

1800 K Street NW
Suite 200
Washington, DC 20006
202.380.3120
202.380.3128 (Fax)

Zimmer Gunsul Frasca Partnership

Perkins Coie LLP
Portland, Oregon

One of Seattle's oldest law firms, Perkins Coie has grown dramatically since 1912, engaging over 600 attorneys serving the corporate world in 14 offices in the United States and China. The thriving Portland office, which has provided legal services to clients in Oregon and beyond for over 20 years, has more than doubled in size during the past seven years. Having outgrown its existing downtown office, the firm used its recent move as the opportunity to completely redesign its physical environment for 80 lawyers and 50 support staff members. The new, three-and-one-half level, 67,000-square-foot office, designed by Zimmer Gunsul Frasca Partnership, portrays Perkins Coie as a world-class provider of legal services without the traditional imagery of the legal profession. Terrazzo floors, metal and glass panels, and a skylighted open stair that connects the four levels are among the exquisitely detailed, high-end finishes and classic modern furnishings that emphatically define the space as a 21st-century environment.

Top: Main reception.
Far left: Small conference room.
Left: Conference center corridor.
Opposite: Lobby and connecting stair.
Photography: Nick Merrick © Hedrich Blessing.

Zimmer Gunsul Frasca Partnership

U.S. Consulate General
New Office Building
Istanbul, Turkey

Although the Palazzo Corpi, an 1882 landmark in Istanbul's historic Beyoglu district, housed the U.S. Consulate General in opulence from 1907 to 2003, the Consul General and his staff are now located 45 minutes outside the city. Fortunately, the Overseas Building Operations, led by General Charles E. Williams, built a new diplomatic compound on a 23-acre hilltop overlooking the Bosphorus in the Istinye Valley. It features such facilities as the two-level, 97,000-square-foot office complex, designed by Zimmer Gunsul Frasca Partnership, that pro-

vides an attractive and effective working environment as well as a more secure one. Outside, the building projects the U.S. diplomatic presence, acknowledges Istanbul's civic buildings, and blends with the adjacent neighborhood. The central courtyard, finished in stone paving, ornamental plantings and seating alcoves, plays a pivotal role by organizing the Consulate's various departments, supporting multiple uses and facilitating circulation. Inside, the lobby, offices and cafeteria are designed as modern, International-style

pavilions with natural materials, classic furnishings, custom lighting and restrained colors that complement an extensive art program. Notes Patrick Collins, Branch Chief, U.S. Dept. of State Bureau of Overseas Building Operations, "The extraordinary drama of the site is most effectively integrated in the building concept."

Top: Conference.
Above: Reception.
Above right: Office.
Right: Office waiting.
Opposite: Cafeteria.
Photography: Christian Richters.

Zimmer Gunsul Frasca Partnership

University of California, San Diego
Rebecca & John Moores UCSD Cancer Center
San Diego, California

Having the opportunity to operate a surgical robot, sample food that may prevent cancer and hear about the newest findings in cancer prevention, all under the same roof, is no longer a cherished dream at the University of California, San Diego. The completion of the new, five-level, 264,063-square-foot Rebecca & John

Moores UCSD Cancer Center, designed by Zimmer Gunsul Frasca Partnership, has launched an award-winning, multi-disciplinary facility for world-class basic science, translational research and clinical care that unites existing programs once scattered across the UCSD campus. With researchers, clinicians, prevention

specialists and educators working together in a "bench-to-bedside" approach to conquering cancer, cancer patients can receive all their outpatient care and much of their education about the disease and its prevention within one facility, while scientists, physicians and students find interacting and exchanging information to be

easy and informal.
M. Boone Hellmann, FAIA, assistant vice chancellor and campus architect for UCSD, concludes his praise for the Cancer Center by observing, "I have always held Zimmer Gunsul Frasca in the highest regard and frankly think they represent a benchmark to which other architectural firms aspire."

Top right: Infusion center.

Top left: Auditorium.

Above: First floor corridor.

Bottom left: Meditation room.

Opposite: Atrium.

Photography: Nick Merrick © Hedrich Blessing.

Zimmer Gunsul Frasca Partnership

Legacy Salmon Creek Hospital
Vancouver, Washington

The first hospital constructed in Vancouver, Washington in years, Legacy Salmon Creek Hospital is raising local expectations for modern health care. Its new, six-story, 470,000-square foot hospital and two medical office buildings of 80,000 square feet and 110,000 square feet, designed by Zimmer Gunsul Frasca Partnership, make a convincing case for patient- and family-focused care. Capitalizing on views of its wooded surroundings, with an ED, ICU, NICU, PACU, operating rooms, labor and delivery rooms, cafeteria, chapel, conference room and cancer center, and a clear and convenient circulation system for patients, visitors and staff, the 220-bed

hospital gives occupants easy access to the resources they need. It also keeps them in contact with the outside world as well as one another, and surrounds them with a functional yet inviting environment. A two-level entry lobby, for example, connects directly to public functions on the third level. A family waiting area central to each floor overlooks a central garden with water features. Each of the single-occupancy patient rooms accommodates family members staying overnight. Staff lounges all provide balconies and views. Interiors of warm colors, sophisticated lighting designed by Frances Krahe, fine materials such as travertine, wood and textiles,

contemporary furnishings and an extensive art program keep the Northwest's legendary long, damp and gray winters at bay.

Above: ICU waiting.

Right top to bottom:
Cafeteria; Emergency Department pediatric waiting; family waiting; gift shop.

Photography: Eckert & Eckert.

Design
with Light.

New York Times Mock-up, College Point Queens, NY
Renzo Piano, Fox & Fowle – Architects
Gensler – Interiors

A New Vision

WindowManagement™ Solutions

Daylighting Controls

Mecho®/5 and Ecoveil™ the first complete

window treatment to receive "Cradle to Cradle™"

Silver Certification from MBDC

www.mechoshade.com

MechoShade®
The Architect's Choice.™
MechoShade Systems, Inc.
718-729-2020 • www.mechoshade.com

DESIGN

QUALITY

SERVICE

A R K

🌿 An environmentally responsible company

Architectural Response
Kollection, Inc.
888.241.7100
www.ark-inc.com

design *is* a choice

seating...desking...tables

MIKADO LOUNGE

KIRKOS
NEW FOR NeoCon® 2006

RADIUS

THE LUCID CHAIR SERIES

AVEA
NEW FOR NeoCon® 2006

AERO

COMpod MEET

ZA
NEW FOR NeoCon® 2006

VERSO

DAVIS®

Davis Furniture Ind. Inc.　　Tel 336 889 2009　　Fax 336 889 0031　　www.davisfurniture.com

Keep your eye on the chip, because things aren't always what they appear to be. Introducing WilsonartHD, all-new High Definition Laminate.
Prepare to be amazed by the beauty & depth in our Bella, Sedona and Deepstar series. See more magic at www.wilsonartlaminate.com/hd or call 800-433-3222.
Pattern Shown: Deepstar Fossil 1812-35

Wilsonart® Laminate

make a statement™

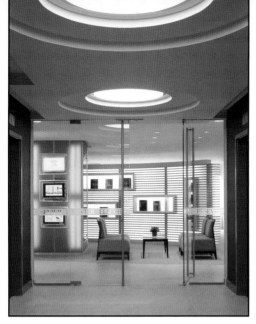

By Roger Yee

It's Face Time at the Office

The traditional concept of the office is under assault as never before

Remember those notorious workaholics, the Japanese? In 1980, Americans alternately feared and pitied the *sarariman* (salaried worker), who toiled for 2,108 hours—versus 1,883 hours for his U.S. counterpart—to help the Land of the Rising Sun propel a tsunami of industrial and consumer goods across the globe. Now fast forward to the 21st century. Surprise: The tables have turned.

Americans are now logging the longest working hours in the industrialized world, turning in 1,825 hours in 2004, considerably more than their counterparts in Japan, with 1,789, Great Britain, with 1,669, Germany, with 1,443, or France, with 1,441. To complicate everyday life in the Land of the Free, growing numbers of American workers are taking the office home and on the road, thanks to wireless Internet connections for their laptops, PDAs and cellular phones. What's going on inside the American office?

To address this question in 2006, a year that marks the seventh volume of Corporate Interiors and its 10th year as an ongoing series, four distinguished architects serving the corporate and institutional world graciously agreed to explore office design from multiple points of view in Corporate Interiors No. 7. Arthur Gensler Jr., FAIA, chairman of Gensler, looked at "What's Design's Impact on the Corporate World?"; Nick Luzietti, AIA, a principal of VOA Architects, considered "Who Needs an Office in the Digital Age?"; Lamarr Reid, AIA, interiors discipline leader of Perkins+Will, asked "Can Design Make Office Workers More Innovative?"; and Dennis Gaffney, AIA, a vice president of RTKL, appraised "How Healthy Is the Office Environment?" Their thoughts provide the substance of this essay.

What they offer readers is a composite portrait of the office environment as a work in progress. Today's office is confronting such issues as the increasing

Naòs System. Studio Cerri & Associati
Pierluigi Cerri
Alessandro Colombo

Photo Mario Carrieri

Naòs System. Studio Cerri & Associati
Pierluigi Cerri
Alessandro Colombo

UNIFOR
149 Fifth Avenue
New York, NY 10010
tel. 212 673 3434
fax 212 673 7317
e-mail: unifor@uniforusa.com

UNIFOR

and institutional leaders, office design is shown to be remarkably adept at supporting management initiatives for a more effective corporate world.

What is design's impact on the corporate world?

Is there anywhere in the physical environment of the corporate world that hasn't been touched by design since the dawn of the information age? "Designers have pretty much changed everything," admits Arthur Gensler Jr., FAIA, chairman of Gensler, the San Francisco-based global design firm he founded 41 years ago. "Not only did we open up space with open planning and Bürolandschaft, we presided over a shift from personal space to group and alternative workspaces, created different environments to serve multiple users, and saw a behavioral change from pomp and circumstance in an historic setting to pragmatism in a contemporary context."

There's been a radical shift in sensibility, Gensler observes. The office is no longer the exclusive province for work. Not only do people commute on a global basis, they don't all have to be in one place to contribute to a collective effort. A major reason for their newfound mobility is that information technology and decision making are now widely dispersed, eliminating the need for highly centralized corporate "battleship" headquarters and campuses, and such venerable institutions as law libraries and ornate executive accommodations.

What has taken the place of these old facilities is decidedly leaner, less rigid and more demanding. "It's scary," Gensler says, "how crucial education is to the corporate jobs that haven't been automated or outsourced. There's been a reduction of two-thirds of the secretaries and other administrative assistants, you see training and teaming on unprecedented levels, command-and-control leadership is phasing out, and work proceeds non-stop. Only the government believes the office operates 9-to-5."

Not surprisingly, the rise in functionality has brought a tough-minded approach to corporate design. CEOs who see the strategic link between design and business—and their numbers are rising—expect

value of collaborative work, the new business focus on innovation, the expanding workplace of information technology, the unprecedented challenge of the global economy, and the search for work-life balance in the absence of job security. Architecture and interior design cannot solve these issues alone, of course. But as a strategic tool wielded by knowledgeable business

design to help them build strong corporate cultures, differentiate one organization from another, adapt to change, facilitate fast action, and support contrarian thinking. Even so, Gensler notes, "We're not encouraged to develop extraordinary spaces for business. Corporate leaders no longer see the value of signature office buildings. They appreciate quality and timelessness, but feel a facility that is highly designed lacks flexibility." Goodbye, Taj Mahal. Hello, Starbucks.

Who needs an office in the digital age?

For an instant demonstration on how technology is reshaping modern life, Nick Luzietti, AIA, a principal of VOA Architects, a Chicago-based design firm with three other U.S. offices and one in Sao Paulo, Brazil, grabs an Apple iPod music player. "Advances like this don't always affect the way we work directly," he indicates. "But look at how quickly we've adopted the idea that you can walk around with 10,000 songs in your pocket." It's an attitude that could revolutionize business recordkeeping someday, he adds.

On the other hand, the need to communicate, aided and abetted by technology, transportation, and social and economic forces, remains a great driver of office design. "We took people out of private spaces beginning in the late 1960s so they could communicate," Luzietti recalls. "But the open-plan office proved to be all-or-nothing. Now we have hybrid spaces that give you privacy when you need it. Still, the need to deal with people face-to-face is the basic reason the office exists."

Some workers value "face time" a lot less than others. But the inability of businesses to measure employees strictly by the results of their work makes them reluctant to stop monitoring everyone within an office environment, Luzietti concedes. Nevertheless, some activities, such as data entry, order processing and direct sales, are already being conducted within workers' own homes, such alternative workplaces as call centers, satellite offices, and "hotelling" and "touchdown" areas in offices, on the road and in customers' premises.

More effective decision-making by critical personnel should keep the office environment at the heart of business operations. Though videoconferencing and e-mail are well established, neither is a substitute for high-level encounters that require the establishment of close rapport and mutual trust. Can offices become more effective as places to meet? Luzietti insists they will. "Younger employees want better offices with more amenities," he points out, "and they'll soon have the upper hand as their numbers drop below the economy's demands for entry level workers."

E 2

designed by
J. Wade Beam and
Victor I. Dziekiewicz

FURNITURE / COMMUNICATION / INNOVATION

800-708-9991   773-772-3700   FCI-OFFICE.COM

Can design make office workers more innovative?

One of the benefits for Lamarr Reid, AIA, of having worked in both architectural practice and corporate facility management is that the interiors discipline leader of Perkins+Will, a Chicago-based international design firm, can comfortably walk 360 degrees around design problems. "I get to mix up design, real estate and corporate strategy in my work," he cheerfully observes. His balanced point of view results in a refreshingly pragmatic approach to the business world's current interest in innovation.

Reid is well aware that creative work often thrives in collaborative environments run by outstanding employees with people skills. Interestingly, he believes new business groups don't absolutely need a specially designed environment. "If they're motivated," he claims, "they can work everywhere."

Here's where the practical corporate strategist meets the creative architect. Reid asserts that matching a space with the way its people work is how office design can best help workers to be more innovative. "Openness isn't ideal for everybody," he says. "If there's a preponderance of head-down work, you'll need private offices. People who spend a lot of time doodling want to do it in privacy. The 'right' approach to the work environment depends on corporate cultures, work patterns and individual work styles."

Reluctant as Reid is to offer generalizations, he admits that the hospitality industry offers inspiration for offices. Hotel and restaurant dining rooms, conference centers and guest accommodations, for example, yield useful design models. Food service is especially valuable, he explains, for breaking down barriers and establishing an informal comfort level so everyone can work as a group and focus on a project.

So why is the garage such an appealing symbol for innovative work? From Reid's vantage point, "It's an unstructured and informal environment. There's no visual language associated with it that you must conform to. Its freedom and loft-like quality are yours without limitations. Who wouldn't like that?"

How healthy is the office environment?

Attention, workaholics. Could your office be making you sick? Dennis Gaffney, AIA, a vice president of RTKL, a Baltimore-based design firm with offices worldwide, is intrigued that technology is both cause and cure for numerous office-based problems of emotional and physical health.

Remarkable Walls

Novawall® meets complex design requirements, has sustainable attributes, and contributes to several LEED™ credits.

On the whole, Gaffney finds technology a plus for employers and employees alike. "Freedom of movement in the workplace, thanks to the connectivity of information technology, offers us genuine relief from work-related stress," he states. "I think most of us would like to leave the office at 5 and continue working at home after 9. Technology lets us stay connected while reducing the time we must spend face-to-face with colleagues. But we still need direct contact. Human nature doesn't change."

Common office environmental hazards and stressors persist, Gaffney acknowledges, but he's confident that better planning and maintenance will help.

• Much office furniture still ignores ergonomics, yet designers and companies are aware of such dangers as repetitive stress disorders.

• Though poor maintenance compromises air quality in older facilities, the situation is greatly improved in new ones.

• Offices still lack sufficient natural lighting.

• Color's power to influence activity remains untapped.

• A lack of variety in office space continues to deny relief to workers who sit for hours at their computers.

In a happy confluence of science, technology and business, "going green" through environmental design is getting a lot easier. "Progress is being made on many fronts," Gaffney finds. "For example, manufacturers of furnishings and building products are taking the lead in incorporating ergonomics and removing volatile organic compounds. Building codes are raising the level of indoor air quality. Owners and operators of facilities are taking maintenance more se-

Hardwood furniture from Harden pleases the most responsible environmentalists—including the one in you.

Non-toxic and natural, American hardwoods are among the most sustainable materials on earth. Unlike composites or synthetics, which take enormous amounts of energy to produce, hardwoods use only the sun to grow.

Harden is acclaimed for its expert management of 20,000+ acres of black cherry, maple and other native species, which it harvests selectively—one or two trees per acre, near the end of their natural lifespan. The forest remains a diverse, mature habitat, and replenishes itself three times faster than it is used.

From this forest, Harden Contract hand-crafts contemporary and traditional designs that bring warmth to any

Harden Office. The natural selection

aesthetic, and can be refinished and reused for generations, making waste a dim, distant prospect.

HARDEN contract

www.hardencontract.com 315.675.3600

riously. Like the ADA (Americans with Disabilities Act), environmental design is becoming part of our daily routine." Is business becoming altruistic about environmental issues? Not really. "Employers are willing to pay for a 'green' office to get happier, healthier and more productive employees," Gaffney suggests, "even if they don't take the LEED route (certification by the U.S. Green Building Council) to achieve it."

Welcome to your shared office

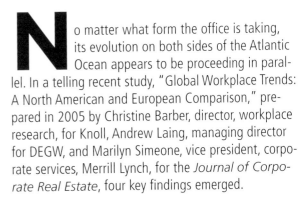

No matter what form the office is taking, its evolution on both sides of the Atlantic Ocean appears to be proceeding in parallel. In a telling recent study, "Global Workplace Trends: A North American and European Comparison," prepared in 2005 by Christine Barber, director, workplace research, for Knoll, Andrew Laing, managing director for DEGW, and Marilyn Simeone, vice president, corporate services, Merrill Lynch, for the *Journal of Corporate Real Estate*, four key findings emerged.

Space to support collaborative work is increasing, the space allocated to individuals is decreasing, telecommuting and working at home are growing, and the use of technologies to support collaboration, connectivity and distributed working is expanding. The study suggests a "tipping point" has been reached that will accelerate changes to the traditional concept of the workplace.

"Space is about control," observes Knoll's Barber. "Most office workers understand this. And young workers are driving us towards a new, interactive and creative social space where they want to work."

Members of Generation Y, informally defined as the cohort born between 1978-2000, will not see their ideal space emerge overnight, to be sure. In their study, Barber, Laing and Simeone point out that the percentage of floor space dedicated to the individual relative to meeting and group activity is 80/20 today, and will change to 60/40 over the next five years. But this still represents a doubling of space for collaborative work, placing Generation Y workers in more environments with less physical boundaries, just the kind of setting these multi-tasking individuals relish. When they need privacy that stops short of full-height walls and doors, they erect electronic barriers.

entourage for conference

Older colleagues may want to watch their backs as the transition towards greater public and communal areas gathers momentum. The Global Workplace Trends study finds that not only will the size of individual or dedicated workspaces diminish over the next five years, so will the overall amount of floor area allocated to individuals. Ironically, everyone in the organizational hierarchy seems likely to share the sense of loss. In North America, executives will see their private offices shrink from 237 to 213 square feet, a 10 percent drop, and secretaries will see their work stations retreat from 68 to 65 square feet, a four percent decline. Similar developments are projected for Europe.

Working at home is no longer confined to sick employees or employees who must tend ailing children or parents, and the organizations in Barber, Laing and Simeone's study have some 15 percent of staff working from home or telecommuting at least one or two days a week. Is the office in danger of emptying out? Not yet. Over the next five years, respondents to the study expect employees working at home full time to grow to an average of eight percent of the work force. Already, they report that two percent of staff lacks their own dedicated work spaces, with the proportion expected to reach over 10 percent in five years as hoteling and free address gain acceptance. Still, it's no mystery where most employees will be most of the time.

That middle-aged workers are among the most enthusiastic users of laptops, PDAs and cellular phones with wireless Internet connections illustrates how profoundly technologies are penetrating our society and supporting collaboration, connectivity and distrib-

WOOD SOLUTIONS
FOR BUSINESS
ENVIRONMENTS

project profile

location: Detroit, Michigan
architect: Ford & Earl
photography: Glen Calvin Moon
product: modified Kubit and FOUNDATION

INTERNATIONAL

315 • 789 • 4400
www.ccninternational.com

uted working. Surprisingly, Global Workplace Trends shows that North Americans and Europeans are not equally enthusiastic about all the changes spurred by information technologies. While nearly 100 percent of European employees have access to group video-conferencing, North American employee use stands at roughly 20 percent. Internet access, by contrast, blankets virtually all workers on both continents.

Since executives control both the rules and the purse strings of the corporate world, their desire to equate workspace with status may survive the waves of evolutionary movements sweeping through today's office. Barber, Laing and Simeone admit as much, indicating that some workspaces will persist in varying according to the levels of their occupants within the hierarchy rather than the nature of their work. (Note how resistant executive pay is to indignant shareholders.) But even at the senior executive level, they point out, shared enclosed offices and non-dedicated spaces are expected to gain favor.

Does this mean your company's CEO will give up his or her spacious corner office when everyone shows up for work this morning, since all that floor area could be used more effectively? Don't count on it. Unless, of course, the CEO proposes the idea.

Credits for projects appearing on pages 264-278

(Clockwise from upper left)

Page 264: Allina Hospitals & Clinics, Minneapolis, MN; Elsevier, Philadelphia, PA; Tai Ping Carpets, New York, NY.

Page 266: Morningstar, Chicago, IL; A Leading Management Consulting Company, Philadelphia, PA; Haynes and Boone, Houston, TX; Mohr Davidow Ventures, Menlo Park, CA.

Page 268: Sun Chemical, Parsippany, NJ; Novo Nordisk, New Brunswick, NJ; Prentice Capital Management, New York, NY; Bloomberg, Chicago, IL.

Page 270: Oceaneering Advanced Technologies Group, Hanover, MD;

Page 272: Corporate Effective Work Practices Program, Charlotte, NC; Michael Salove Company, Philadelphia, PA; Comcast Spotlight, Chicago, IL.

Page 274: Major Financial Institution, Rolling Meadows, IL (two images); Hennepin County Brookdale Regional Center, Brooklyn Center, MN; German Marshall Fund of the United States, Washington, DC; Waste Management, Scottsdale, AZ.

Page 276: Brazos Private Equity Partners, Dallas, TX; THQ, Agoura Hills, CA; Credit Suisse Private Advisors, Miami, FL; United States Consulate General, Istanbul, Turkey; Brazos Private Equity Partners, Dallas, TX.

Page 278: Metrovest Equities, New York, NY; Cinergy Corporation, Cincinnati, OH.

Harter Shapes, Forum Collection
Design by Timothy deFiebre

Teso Executive
Design by Prof. Horst Bruenint and Partners

Kion
Design by Indecom/Just Meyer

Photography by Dylan Cross Photographer, NYC

Workin' hard or hardly workin'?

Spare your employees the lame jokes. With a Harter furnished office, you can achieve that "hip boss" reputation without them.

 at the heart of the solution®

800.543.5449 harter.com

 harter [♥]®

STRUCTURETONE
Organization

Delivering Success
Your Project. Your Needs.
Our Construction Expertise.

The preferred interiors construction manager for consummate quality—making owners' and architects' visions a reality.

Carson Guest: Architect/Gabriel Benzur: Photographer

Resources*

655 Broadway, San Diego, CA
Design Firm: Carrier Johnson
General Contractors: Webcor Builders
Lighting Consultants: Horton Lees Brogden
Lighting Design

Allina Hospitals & Clinics - Corporate Headquarters
Design Firm: Perkins+Will
Furniture: Brayton, Herman Miller
Carpets & Flooring: Constantine, Mohawk
Fabrics: Knoll, Maharam
Lighting: Lightolier
Ceilings: Armstrong
Wallcoverings and Paint: Knoll, Sherwin-Williams
Window Treatments: Hunter Douglas
General Contractors: Ryan Construction
Lighting Consultants: LKPB Engineers

American Airlines Admirals Club - JFK Int'l Airport
Design Firm: Spillis Candela DMJM
Furniture: Brayton, Charles Alan, Ekitta
Carpets & Flooring: Collins & Aikman, Imagine Tiles, Walker Zanger
Fabrics: Knoll, Maharam, Spinneybeck
Wallcoverings and Paint: Architectural Systems, Blumenthal, ICI Paints, Maya Romanoff, Southwest Progressive Enterprises
General Contractors: Cardet Construction Co. Inc.

AstraZeneca - Government Affairs Department Offices
Design Firm: Kling
Furniture: Brayton, Davis, Nienkamper, Steelcase
Carpets & Flooring: Arc Stone, Armstrong, Daltile, Forbo, Shaw
Lighting: Bartco, Gotham, Kurt Versen, Lithonia, RSA Lighting, Selux
Ceilings: Armstrong
Wallcoverings and Paint: Benjamin Moore, Daltile, Designtex, Duroplex, Maharam, Zolatone
Window Treatments: Maharam
General Contractors: Sigel Construction Corporation
Lighting Consultants: Kling

AstraZeneca - Lobby Renovation
Design Firm: Francis Cauffman Foley Hoffmann Architects, Ltd.
Furniture: Steelcase
Lighting: Louis Poulsen
Ceilings: Armstrong
Wallcoverings and Paint: Rulon Co.

BankAtlantic Corporate Center
Design Firm: Spillis Candela DMJM
Furniture: Baker, Brayton, Kartell
Carpets & Flooring: Bentley, Invision, Milliken
Fabrics: Carnegie, Knoll, Maharram, Unika Vaev
Lighting: Belfer, Contemporary Light Fixtures
Ceilings: Interlam
Wallcoverings and Paint: Benjamin Moore, Pittsburgh Paints
General Contractors: Itasca Construction Associates, Inc.

bkm OfficeWorks
Design Firm: Carrier Johnson
Furniture: bkm OfficeWorks, Steelcase
Carpets & Flooring: Harris-Tarkett, Mannington, Shaw, Stratica
Lighting: Focal Point, Lightolier
Ceilings: Armstrong
Wallcoverings and Paint: Allstate, Benjamin Moore
General Contractors: Bycor General Contractors

Bloomberg L.P. - Chicago
Design Firm: Perkins+Will
Furniture: Catifa, Knoll, Vitra
Carpets & Flooring: Lees, Tate
Fabrics: Knoll, Spinneybeck
Lighting: Gotham, Kurt Versen, Selux
Ceilings: Armstrong
Wallcoverings and Paint: Art Diffusion, Benjamin Moore, Knoll
Window Treatments: MechoShade
General Contractors: Clone Construction
Lighting Consultants: Perkins+Will

Bloomberg L.P.
Design Firm: CBT/Childs Bertman Tseckares, Inc.
Furniture: Alea, Arper, B&B Italia, Knoll, Knoll Studio, Matteo Grassi, Moroso, Walter Knoll
Carpets & Flooring: Collins & Aikman, Fritztile, Shaw

Fabrics: Knoll, Kvadrat
Lighting: Xenon, Zumtobel
Ceilings: Armstrong, Ceilings Plus, Echophon, USG
Wallcoverings and Paint: Acoustone, Benjamin Moore, InStyle, Sherwin Williams
Window Treatments: MechoShade
General Contractors: Commodore Builders
Lighting Consultants: D. Schweppe

Brown Rudnick Berlack Israels
Design Firm: Gensler
Furniture: Herman Miller, Knoll, Walker Zanger, Wall/Goldfinger, Zographos
Carpets & Flooring: Bloomsburg, Stone Source
Fabrics: Maharam
Ceilings: Decoustics
General Contractors: Turner Construction Company
Lighting Consultants: Sbld Studio

Choate Hall & Stewart LLP
Design Firm: CBT/Childs Bertman Tseckares, Inc.
Furniture: A. Rudin, Datesweiser, Donghia, Gerard, HBF, Keilhauer, Mark Richey Woodworking, Q Collection
Carpets & Flooring: Atlas, Bentley, Berti Wood Flooring, Constantine, Fortune Contract, Refin Creamiche
Fabrics: Bergamo, Brunschwig, Classic Cloth, Donghia, Moore & Giles, Sina Pearson, Spinneybeck, Zimmer & Rhode
Lighting: Color Kinetics, Focal Point, Gotham, Litecontrol
Ceilings: Armstrong
Wallcoverings and Paint: Benjamin Moore, Henry Calvin, Knoll, Sherwin Williams
General Contractors: Payton Construction
Lighting Consultants: D. Schweppe

Cinergy Headquarters
Design Firm: Champlin/Haupt Architects
Furniture: Cabot Wrenn, David Edward, HBF
Carpets & Flooring: Bentley, Designweave
Fabrics: Gretchen Bellinger, HBF, Jack Lenor Larson, Sina Pearson, Spinneybeck
Lighting: Lithonia, Karlin
Ceilings: Armstrong
Wallcoverings and Paint: Carnegie, Sherwin Williams

*An Incomplete list of major sources.
For more information please call design firms.

282

Window Treatments: MechoShade
General Contractors: Hunt Builders

Cinergy Traders
Design Firm: Champlin/Haupt Architects
Furniture: Bernhardt, Haworth, Herman Miller, Knoll, SoHo
Carpets & Flooring: Collins & Aikman, Invision, Masland, Shaw
Fabrics: Designtex, Knoll, Maharam, Pallas, Spinneybeck, Xorel
Lighting: Boyd, Flos, IE Architectural, Italiana Luce, Litecontrol, Mazzega, Prescolite, SPI
Ceilings: Armstrong
Wallcoverings and Paint: Designtex, Innovations, JM Lynne, Knoll
Window Treatments: Levelor
General Contractors: Turner Construction

Cleary Gottlieb Steen & Hamilton LLP
Design Firm: Gerner Kronick + Valcarcel, Architects, PC
Furniture: Herman Miller, Knoll, Walter P. Sauer
Carpets & Flooring: Bentley, Bloomberg, Legno Veneto
Fabrics: Knoll, Maharam, Spinneybeck
Lighting: Alkco, Legion, Lightolier, Light Solutions, Mark Lighting, Nessen, Nulux, RSA, Starfire Lighting
Ceilings: Armstrong, Newmat VGA, Ltd.
Wallcoverings and Paint: Benjamin Moore, Fresco
Window Treatments: MechoShade
General Contractors: Bovis Lend Lease Interiors, Inc.
Lighting Consultants: HDLC Architectural Lighting Design

Corporate Headquarters
Design Firm: Spillis Candela DMJM
Furniture: ICF, Knoll
Carpets & Flooring: Constantine, Milliken
General Contractors: Hourigan Construction
Lighting Consultants: Bliss Fasman

Corporate Synergies
Design Firm: H. Hendy Associates
Furniture: Geiger, Herman Miller
Carpets & Flooring: Bolon, Crema Marfil Marble, Shaw
Fabrics: Jhane Barnes, Maharam
Lighting: Bruck, Lithonia, Systemlux

Ceilings: Armstrong
Wallcoverings and Paint: Zolatone

The Coyle Company
Design Firm: Margulies & Associates
Furniture: Kimball, Knoll, Leland, Lowenstein
Carpets & Flooring: Armstrong, Designweave
Fabrics: Knoll, Spinneybeck, Unika Vaev
Lighting: Bruck, Focal Point, Litecontrol, Portfolio, Visa
Ceilings: USG
Wallcoverings and Paint: Benjamin Moore
Window Treatments: Lumicor
General Contractors: Execuspace Construction
Lighting Consultants: Boston Light Source

Digitas Indirect Marketing Company - Chicago
Design Firm: Perkins+Will
Furniture: Herman Miller, Inscape
Carpets & Flooring: Interface, Lees, Mannington
Lighting: Focal Point, Juno, Lightolier
Ceilings: USG
Wallcoverings and Paint: American Olean, Benjamin Moore, Shannon, Wolf Gordon
General Contractors: Clone Construction
Lighting Consultants: Perkins+Will

Dougherty Financial Group
Design Firm: Perkins+Will
Furniture: HBF, Holly Hunt
Carpets & Flooring: Aueky Angelo, Wengewood Flooring
Fabrics: Great Plains, Gretchen Bellinger, Holly Hunt
Lighting: Boyd, Holly Hunt, Lightolier
Wallcoverings and Paint: Knoll, Maharam, Sherwin-Williams
General Contractors: RJM Construction
Lighting Consultants: Perkins+Will

Elevation Partners
Design Firm: BraytonHughes Design Studios
Furniture: DFM, Herman Miller, Keilhauer, Knoll
Carpets & Flooring: Invision, J&J Industries
Lighting: Artemide, Lightolier, Linear, Kurt Versen, Phoenix Day
Ceilings: Armstrong, USG
Wallcoverings and Paint: Benjamin Moore, Unika Vaev

General Contractors: Devcon Construction, Inc.
Lighting Consultants: HLB Lighting Design

eSecLending
Design Firm: Margulies & Associates
Furniture: Herman Miller, Lowenstein
Carpets & Flooring: Constantine, Forbo
Fabrics: Maharam
Lighting: LBC Lighting, Sonoma, Translight
Ceilings: MFGR
Wallcoverings and Paint: Benjamin Moore, Invironments, Maharam
Window Treatments: MechoShade
General Contractors: Spaulding & Slye

Ethicon, Inc.
Design Firm: Champlin/Haupt Architects
Flooring: American Olean
Lighting: Bruck, Lightolier
Ceilings: Armstrong
Wallcoverings and Paint: ICI
General Contractors: Resource One

Ethicon, Inc. - Cafeteria & Conference Center
Design Firm: Francis Cauffman Foley Hoffmann Architects, Ltd.
Furniture: BIX Seating
Carpets & Flooring: Intalgraniti, Interface
Lighting: Calculite
Ceilings: Armstrong
Wallcoverings and Paint: Benjamin Moore, Zolatone
General Contractors: CYMA Construction
Lighting Consultants: in-house

Fifth Third
Design Firm: Champlin/Haupt Architects
Furniture: Brayton, Haworth, Keilhauer, KI, Landscapeforms, Nova, Steelcase
Carpets & Flooring: Armstrong, Chromtech, Milliken, Shaw
Fabrics: Designtex
Lighting: Ennergie, Litecontrol
Wallcoverings and Paint: Devoc, MDC, Scuffmaster, Victrex, Wolf Gordon
General Contractors: Belvedere
Lighting Consultants: KLH Engineers

Highway

Design: Martin Ballendat

DaupHin

HumanDesign® Group

Fox Rothschild LLP
Design Firm: Francis Cauffman Foley Hoffmann Architects, Ltd.
Furniture: Aussie Chairs, David Edward, Lolita Tables
Carpets & Flooring: Shaw
Fabrics: Bernhardt, Spinneybeck
Ceilings: USG
Wallcoverings and Paint: Maharam
Window Treatments: MechoShade

Herman Miller Showroom
Design Firm: H. Hendy Associates
Furniture: Geiger, HBF, Herman Miller,
Carpets & Flooring: Collins & Aikman, Gammapar, Plynyl
Fabrics: Edelman Leather, Jhane Barnes, Luna, Momentum, Unika Vaev
Lighting: Bruck, Global Lighting, Lightolier, Modernica, Nelson
Wallcoverings and Paint: Modular Arts, Zolatone
General Contractors: Turelk

nfinity Broadcasting
Design Firm: Partridge Architects
Furniture: Herman Miller
Carpets & Flooring: Armstrong, Shaw
Fabrics: Knoll
Lighting: Gammalux, Lightolier, Prima Lighting
Ceilings: Armstrong
Wallcoverings and Paint: Benjamin Moore, Maharam, Wolf Gordon
General Contractors: Lakash Constructors Inc.

Knight Capital Group, Inc.
Design Firm: Ted Moudis, Inc.
Furniture: Baker, Brunschwig Fils, John Boone, Woodtronics
Carpets & Flooring: Constantine, Milliken
Fabrics: Bergamo, Edelman Leather, Holly Hunt
Lighting: Lithonia, Mark Lighting
Ceilings: Ecophon
Wallcoverings and Paint: Benjamin Moore, Carnegie, Designtex, Jim Thompson
General Contractors: StructureTone
Lighting Consultants: Hillman DiBernardo

Korn/Ferry International
Design Firm: Wolcott Architecture • Interiors
Carpets & Flooring: Durkam, Karastan, Travertine
Lighting: Eureka

Ceilings: Armstrong, Decoustics
Wallcoverings and Paint: Knoll
Window Treatments: HBF, MechoShade
General Contractors: Stanhope Company
Lighting Consultants: in-house

L.A.R.D. Investments, L.P.
Design Firm: H. Hendy Associates
Furniture: Herman Miller, Jofco, Martin Brattrud, OFS
Carpets & Flooring: Durkam, Lonseal, Patcraft, Permagrain, Shaw
Fabrics: Deepa, Luna
Lighting: Armstrong
Wallcoverings and Paint: Maharam, Zolatone
Lighting Consultants: Tech Lighting

LaSalle Bank Chicago Marathon
Design Firm: VOA Associates Inc.
Furniture: Knoll, Vitra
Carpets & Flooring: Interface
Fabrics: Knoll, Maharam
Lighting: Kurt Versen
Ceilings: Anning Johnson
Wallcoverings and Paint: Anning Johnson, Benjamin Moore
General Contractors: Valenti Builders
Lighting Consultants: VOA Associates

Major Financial Institution
Design Firm: H. Hendy Associates
Furniture: Herman Miller, Lowenstein
Carpets & Flooring: Bolon, Cambridge, Shaw, Stone, Zodiaq
Fabrics: Luna, Maharam, Pollack
Lighting: Bruck, Design Within Reach, Eureka, Zumtobel
Ceilings: USG
Wallcoverings and Paint: Zolatone
General Contractors: Pepper Construction

Martin Patterson Global Advisors
Design Firm: Ted Moudis Associates
Furniture: David Edward, HBF, Steelcase, Tuohy, Wyeth
Carpets & Flooring: Constantine, Karastan
Fabrics: Designtex, Gretchen Bellinger
Lighting: Kurt Versen, Lucifer, Selux, Zumtobel
Ceilings: USG
Wallcoverings and Paint: Edelman Leather, Spinneybeck

Window Treatments: Sol-R-Shade
General Contractors: J.T. Magen

McNeil Consumer & Specialty Pharmaceuticals - Administration Building B - New Workplace Transformation
Design Firm: Francis Cauffman Foley Hoffmann Architects, Ltd.
Furniture: Brayton, Herman Miller
Carpets & Flooring: Atlas, Constantine
Fabrics: Designtex, Studio Line, One+One
Lighting: Focal Point, Lightolier
Ceilings: Armstrong, USG
Wallcoverings and Paint: Designtex, One+One, MAB
General Contractors: W.M. Drayton & Company

Metrovest Equities
Design Firm: Ted Moudis Associates
Furniture: Bernhardt, HBF, Jofco, Troy
Carpets & Flooring: ASI Flooring, Bloomberg, Constantine
Fabrics: Bernhardt Leather
Lighting: Mark Lighting, Zumtobel
Ceilings: Armstrong
Wallcoverings and Paint: Benjamin Moore
Window Treatments: Sol-R-Shade
General Contractors: J.G.N. Construction Corp.
Michael Salove Company
Design Firm: Partridge Architects
Furniture: Chiasso, DWR, Stylex, Teknion, 3 Form, West Elm
Carpets & Flooring: Armstrong, Shaw
Lighting: Artemide, Bruck, Finelite
Wallcoverings and Paint: Eykon, Sherwin Williams
General Contractors: D'Lauro & Rodgers

Mohr, Davidow Ventures
Design Firm: BraytonHughes Design Studios
Furniture: Bright, DFM, Geiger, Herman Miller, Keilhauer, Nevins, Wood Industries
Carpets & Flooring: Forbo, Invision, J&J Indusries, Soinhofen
Wallcoverings and Paint: Ann Sacks, Benjamin Moore, Designtex, Olea Plaster, Unika Vaev, Wood Tech Industries
General Contractors: Hallmark Construction
Lighting Consultants: HLB Lighting Design

Morgan Stanley
Design Firm: Roger Ferris + Partners
Furniture: Steelcase

Jofco

[Collective® Space, Office and Lounge. Design at Work.]

j

800-235-6326   furniture@jofco.com   www.jofco.com | Design: Lynda Chesser and Bill Schacht

Carpets & Flooring: Bentley, Forbo
Lighting: Edison Price, Eliptipar, Zumtobel
Ceilings: Decoustics, Echophon, USG
Wallcoverings and Paint: Benjamin Moore, Maharam, Tnemec
General Contractors: Plaza Construction
Lighting Consultants: Kugler Tillotson & Associates

Morgenthaler Ventures
Design Firm: BraytonHughes Design Studios
Furniture: Halcon, HBF, Holly Hunt, McGuire, Steelcase, Tuohy, Vecta
Carpets & Flooring: Constantine
Lighting: Kurt Versen
Ceilings: Armstrong
Wallcoverings and Paint: Benjamin Moore
Window Treatments: MechoShade
General Contractors: Hallmark Construction
Lighting Consultants: HLB Lighting Design

Morningstar
Design Firm: Lee Stout Inc.
Furniture: Driade, Herman Miller, Kartell, Metro, Office Specialties, Shaker Workshops, Steelcase, Unifor, Vecta, Vitra
Carpets & Flooring: Interface
Fabrics: Designtex
Lighting: Artemide, Flos, Focal Point, Lightolier, Luce Plan
Ceilings: Tectum
General Contractors: Interior Alterations
Lighting Consultants: Jim Conti Lighting

Morrison & Foerster
Design Firm: Carrier Johnson
Furniture: Geiger, HBF, Kimball, Krug, Nucraft, Steelcase
Carpets & Flooring: Crossville, Emser Tile, Mannington, Masland
Fabrics: Architex, Bernhardt, Designtex, Maharam, Momentum, Sina Pearson, Spinneybeck
Lighting: Kurt Versen, Ledalite, Modular, Tango, Zumtobel
Ceilings: Armstrong
Wallcoverings and Paint: ICI
Window Treatments: MechoShade
General Contractors: Swinerton Builders
Lighting Consultants: JS Nolan & Associates Lighting Design, LLC

Nokia, Atlanta
Design Firm: Gensler
Furniture: Haworth, Herman Miller
Carpets & Flooring: Interface
Ceilings: Armstrong
General Contractors: Humphries and Company

Northland Investment Corporation
Design Firm: Margulies & Associates
Furniture: Bernhardt, HBF, Jofco
Carpets & Flooring: Rossi USA
Lighting: Artemide
Wallcoverings and Paint: Sherwin Williams
General Contractors: Chapman Construction

Office Environments of New England
Design Firm: CBT/Childs Bertman Tseckares, Inc.
Furniture: B&B Italia, Bernhardt, Steelcase, Zanotta
Carpets & Flooring: Bianco Laragnina Marble, Collins & Aikman, Constantine, Daltile, QC Cemtint
Fabrics: Bernhardt, Brayton, Edelman Leather, Gretchen Bellinger, Maharam
Lighting: Glenlyte Companies, Lightolier
Ceilings: Armstrong, GWB
Wallcoverings and Paint: Bio-shield, C2, Schreuder
Window Treatments: Mechoshade
General Contractors: Turner Construction
Lighting Consultants: Schweppe Lighting Design

Ospraie Management LLC
Design Firm: Ted Moudis Associates
Furniture: Allsteel, Bernhardt, Dateswiser, Dauphin, Herman Miller, Keilhauer
Carpets & Flooring: Interface
Fabrics: Luna, Spinneybeck
Lighting: Zumtobel
Ceilings: Armstrong, Decoustics
Wallcoverings and Paint: Benjamin Moore
General Contractors: Lewis and Kennedy

PB Capital Corporation
Design Firm: Gerner Kronick + Valcarcel, Architects, PC
Furniture: Fentoni, MAL Dealer
Carpets & Flooring: Lees, Terrazzo
Fabrics: Designtex, Maharam
Lighting: Louis Poulsen, Zumtobel

Ceilings: Armstrong
Wallcoverings and Paint: Benjamin Moore
Window Treatments: MechoShade
General Contractors: Bovis Lend Lease Interiors, Inc.
Lighting Consultants: Jim Panichella International Lights

Pepper Hamilton LLP
Design Firm: Kling
Furniture: Bernhardt, Bright, HBF, National Casegoods, Steelcase, Walt Goldfinger
Carpets & Flooring: Armstrong, Monterey, Stone Source
Fabrics: HBF, Larson, Pollack
Lighting: Baldinger
Ceilings: Armstrong
Wallcoverings and Paint: Benjamin Moore, Maharam, Wolf Gordon
Window Treatments: MechoShade, Pollack
General Contractors: Erickson & Sons
Lighting Consultants: Kling

Perkins Coie, LLP
Design Firm: Zimmer Gunsul Frasca Partnership
Furniture: Casa Moroso, Davis, Design Link, Divani, Ekitta, Herman Miller, Howe, IFC, Knoll, Malik
Carpets & Flooring: Atlas, Duraloc MG, DuPont, Durkan, Forbo, Solutia Ultron
Fabrics: Maharam, Spinneybeck
Lighting: A-Light, Artemide, Belfer, ELP, MP, Zumtobel
Ceilings: Armstrong, Decoustics
Wallcoverings and Paint: Designtex, Miller Paints, Rodda
Window Treatments: MechoShade
General Contractors: Skanska Building USA
Lighting Consultants: Francis Krahe and Associates

Pershing Square Capital Management
Design Firm: Gerner Kronick + Valcarcel, Architects, PC
Furniture: Kresents, Pucci, Tuohy
Carpets & Flooring: Monterey, Timeless Timber
Fabrics: Edelman
Lighting: Baldinger, Lightolier, Linear Lighting, LiteLab
Ceilings: Armstrong
Wallcoverings and Paint: Acme Architectural Walls, Benjamin Moore, Fresco, Scuffmaster, Wolf Gordon

NeoCon® SHOWS

North America's **largest** collection of expositions and conferences for interior design and facilities management ...

IIDEX®/NeoCon® Canada
September 28-29, 2006
The National Trade Centre
Toronto, Ont.

NeoCon® East
October 11-12, 2006
Baltimore Convention Center
Baltimore, Md.

NeoCon® World's Trade Fair
June 11-13, 2007
The Merchandise Mart • Chicago, Ill.

NeoCon® Xpress
September 2007
Los Angeles, Calif.

www.merchandisemart.com 800.677.6278

photography by audia • john dean • felderman keatinge & associates • steve reisch

Window Treatments: MechoShade
General Contractors: Bovis Lend Lease Interiors, Inc.
Lighting Consultants: HDLC Architectural Lighting Design

Pillsbury Winthrop Shaw Pittman
Design Firm: BraytonHughes Design Studios
Furniture: Baker, Bernhardt, Geiger, Humanscale, Keilhauer, Knoll, Woodtech
Carpets & Flooring: Shaw
Ceilings: Eurospan Ceiling System
General Contractors: Devoon Construction
Lighting Consultants: HLB Lighting Design

Prentice Capital
Design Firm: Mojo•Stumer Associates
Furniture: Allsteel, HBF, Tuohy
Carpets & Flooring: Bolyu, Monterey
Fabrics: HBF, Knoll
Lighting: Modulan Lighting, PSM Lighting, Zumtobel
Ceilings: Armstrong
Wallcoverings and Paint: Benjamin Moore
General Contractors: American

Rebecca and John Moores UCSD Cancer Center
Design Firm: Zimmer Gunsul Frasca Partnership
Furniture: Brayton, Janus et Cie, Metro, Steelcase
Carpets & Flooring: Armstrong, Bentley, Masland, Prince Street
Fabrics: Carnegie, Designtex, Knoll, Luna Textiles, Maharam
Lighting: Louis Poulsen, Selux, Zumtobel
Ceilings: Decoustics, USG, Wood Ceilings
Wallcoverings and Paint: Benjamin Moore, Dunn Edwards, ICI Paints, Maharam
Window Treatments: Skyco
General Contractors: McCarthy
Lighting Consultants: Francis Krahe & Associates, Inc.

RK Restaurant
Design Firm: Roger Ferris + Partners
Furniture: Bernhardt, Zanotta
Carpets & Flooring: Pat Morris Tile & Marble
Ceilings: Artisan Sound Control
Wallcoverings and Paint: Benjamin Moore

General Contractors: Wescorp Builders
Lighting Consultants: Engineered Lighting Products

R.R. Donnelley
Design Firm: VOA Associates Inc.
Furniture: ICF, Knoll, Nienkamper, Tuohy
Carpets & Flooring: Constantine, Shaw
Fabrics: Donghia, Holly Hunt, Knoll, Maharam, Unika Vaev
Lighting: Focal Point, Square One
Ceilings: Armstrong
Wallcoverings and Paint: Donghia, Maharam
Window Treatments: Lutron
General Contractors: Leopardo

RW Johnson Pharmaceutical Research Institute
Design Firm: Carrier Johnson
Carpets & Flooring: American Olean, Armstrong, Prince Street
Ceilings: Decoustics, USG
Wallcoverings and Paint: Benjamin Moore, Carnegie, Frazee
General Contractors: Rudolph & Sletten

Salmon Creek Hospital
Design Firm: Zimmer Gunsul Frasca Partnership
Furniture: Allermuir, Brayton, David Edward, Geiger Int'l, Leland, Nemschoo
Carpets & Flooring: Atlas, Interface, Invision, Masland, Plynyl by Chilewich
Fabrics: Brayton, HBF, Knoll, Maharam, Textus, Willowtex
Lighting: LBL, Louis Poulsen
Ceilings: Armstrong, Roulon
Wallcoverings and Paint: Hopper Handcrafter, Miller Paint
Window Treatments: MechoShade
General Contractors: Skanska Building USA
Lighting Consultants: Francis Krahe and Associates

Shire
Design Firm: Champlin/Haupt Architects
Furniture: Cabot Wrenn, Keilhauer, Kimball, National
Carpets & Flooring: Forbo, Shaw
Fabrics: Designtex, Kimball
Lighting: Artemide, Cooper Portfolio, Hampstead, Metalux
Ceilings: Armstrong

Wallcoverings and Paint: Designtex, Knoll, Wolf Gordon
General Contractors: Hunt Builders
Lighting Consultants: KLH Engineers

Sonnemschein Nath & Rosenthal LLP
Design Firm: Gerner Kronick + Valcarcel, Architects, PC
Furniture: Steelcase
Carpets & Flooring: Collins & Aikman, Constantine, Karastan
Fabrics: Designtex
Lighting: Arch Lighting, Delray, Edison Price, Erco, Frisma, Halo, ITRE USA, Legion, Lucifer, National, Nuarc, Portfone, Schmite, Selux, Wila
Ceilings: Armstrong
Wallcoverings and Paint: Benjamin Moore, Fresco, Maharam
Window Treatments: Sol-R-Control
General Contractors: Lehr Construction Corp.
Lighting Consultants: HDLC Architectural Lighting Design, Thompson & Sears Lighting Design

The State Room
Design Firm: Margulies & Associates
Carpets & Flooring: Gammapar, Glacier Glass Tiles
Lighting: Andromeda Intl, Corelite, Eliptipar, Focal Point, Intense Lighting, Lithonia, Lutron, Prudential
Ceilings: USG
Wallcoverings and Paint: Maya Romanoff, Wolf Gordon
General Contractors: Commodore Builders
Lighting Consultants: Boston Light Source

Studley, Inc.
Design Firm: VOA Associates Inc.
Furniture: Allsteel, Davis, Gordon International, Herman Miller, Martin Brandrud
Carpets & Flooring: Armstrong, Bentley, Constantine, Mohawk
Fabrics: Cortina Leather, Knoll
Lighting: Aiko, Cooper Lighting, Focal Point, Lightblock, Tech Lighting, USA Illumination
Ceilings: Armstrong
Wallcoverings and Paint: Benjamin Moore
General Contractors: Interior Construction Group (ICG)

IIDA

INTERNATIONAL INTERIOR DESIGN ASSOCIATION

why iida?

Because while it is all about design, it's also about our Members, professional growth and shaping the future. Take your individual seat and be a part of something greater.

- Opportunities to learn from design leaders.
- Professional networking with over 12,000 Members.
- The chance to shape the future of design through legislative activities.
- Educational opportunities at the Chapter level, including CEUs and NCIDQ prep courses.
- Professional development resources available ONLY to Members.

Visit our website at www.iida.org or call toll free 888.799.IIDA for a membership application today. We're saving you a seat.

The Association for **Design Professionals**

Sun Chemical
Design Firm: Gensler
Furniture: Bernhardt, Geiger Int'l
Carpets & Flooring: Fritz Industries, J&J Industries
Fabrics: Edelman Leather, Holly Hunt
General Contractors: Gale Company
Lighting Consultants: HDLC Architectural Lighting Design

THQ
Design Firm: Wolcott Architecture • Interiors
Furniture: Allsteel
Carpets & Flooring: Shaw
Fabrics: Maharam
Lighting: Delray, Lithonia, Peerless
Ceilings: Armstrong
Wallcoverings and Paint: Knoll
Window Treatments: MechoShade
General Contractors: RCI Builders

Turner Construction - SPG/Special Projects Group
Design Firm: Kling
Furniture: Herman Miller, Knoll, Knoll Studio
Carpets & Flooring: Armstrong, Commercial Floorscape Systems, Constantine, Johnsonite, Lonseal, Shaw
Fabrics: Knoll
Lighting: Louis Poulsen
Ceilings: Armstrong, USG
Wallcoverings and Paint: Benjamin Moore, Knoll, Scuffmaster

Window Treatments: MechoShade
General Contractors: Turner SPG
Lighting Consultants: Kling

U.S. Consulate General, New Office Building, Istanbul, Turkey
Design Firm: Zimmer Gunsul Frasca Partnership
Furniture: Baker, Geiger, Herman Miller, ICF, Knoll, Vecta
Carpets & Flooring: Bloomsburg, Collins & Aikman, Interface, Minteg, Travertine
Fabrics: Carnegie, Knoll, Maharam, Sina Pearson, Spinneybeck
Lighting: Zumtobel
Ceilings: Armstrong
Wallcoverings and Paint: Benjamin Moore, Carnegie, Jack Lenor Larson
Window Treatments: MechoShade
General Contractors: Caddell Construction Co., Inc., ENKA Construction Co.
Lighting Consultants: Fisher Marantz Stone

Venables, Bell & Partners
Design Firm: Gensler
Furniture: Cherner Chair, Geiger Int'l, Herman Miller, Knoll, Teknion, United Furniture of America
Carpets & Flooring: Blue Ridge
Fabrics: Designtex, Unika Vaev
Lighting: Lampa
Ceilings: USG
Lighting Consultants: Architecture & Light

Wallace Roberts & Todd, LLC
Design Firm: Partridge Architects
Furniture: Knoll
Carpets & Flooring: Interface
Fabrics: Maharam
Ceilings: Armstrong
Wallcoverings and Paint: MAB, Maharam
Window Treatments: MechoShade
General Contractors: W.S. Cumby & Son
Lighting Consultants: David Nelson & Associates

Wilmington Trust
Design Firm: Wolcott Architecture • Interiors
Furniture: Seeley Bros.
Carpets & Flooring: JB Marble, Masland
Fabrics: Knoll, Maharam
Lighting: Artemide, Lithonia, Peerless
Ceilings: USG
Wallcoverings and Paint: Frazee, Maharam
Window Treatments: MechoShade
General Contractors: Nexus Construction
Lighting Consultants: in-house

Wolcott Architecture • Interiors - lobby
Design Firm: Wolcott Architecture • Interiors
Furniture: Bernhardt, Knoll, Seeley Bros.
Carpets & Flooring: Bentley, JB Marble, Shaw
Fabrics: Maharam
Lighting: Delray, Intense, Peerlite
Wallcoverings and Paint: ICI
Window Treatments: MechoShade, Phillips Drapery
General Contractors: Gordon Construction
Lighting Consultants: in-house

INTERSECT WEST '07

Introducing **Intersect**West '07

IT'S TIME TO MOBILIZE THE POWER OF OUR INDUSTRY BY INTEGRATING OUR BEST PRODUCTS, PRACTICES AND THINKING

A Leading Edge Intersection
of Ideas, Issues & Trends for
a New Era in Product & Design
for Commercial Environments

February 28 – March 2, 2007
Mandalay Bay Convention Center
Las Vegas, Nevada

IntersectWest will provide the uniting industry
forum that you've been waiting for.

**Register to attend the event and participate
in the conference program at intersectwest.com**

**This premier exhibition will
feature innovative products and
services** at the intersection of
commercial environment design
and development, including:

Accessories

Architectural Products:
Ceilings/Floors/Skylights/Walls

Carpet & Rugs

Finishes: Glass/Leathers/Paints
Stains/Stone/Tile/Vinyls

Furniture: Educational
Healthcare/Hospitality/Outdoor
Restaurant/Retail

Lighting: Task/Ambient

Office: Systems/Casegoods
Tables/Seating/Files
Storage Units

Technology & Security Products

Textiles

**Don't miss the opportunity
to join in this dynamic exchange!**
IntersectWest promises to be
the preeminent, future-focused
event for showcasing the hottest
in leading-edge products, ideas
and services.

**Connect with the latest
information and thinking in:**
Changing Demographics
New Ways of Working
Collaborative Work Environments
Learning and Healing Environments
Integrating Technology
Sustainability
Business in China and the Pacific Rim
New Materials
Color Trends
Security

Sponsored by the Contract Interiors
Marketing Association (CIMA),
a not-for-profit corporation.
The latest information on speakers
& seminars can be found online
at intersectwest.com or by calling
Executive Director Hank de Cillia
at 631.725.2745.

Index by Project

The Designer Series

Visual Reference Publications, Inc.

302 Fifth Avenue, New York, NY 10001
212.279.7000 • Fax 212.279.7014
www.visualreference.com

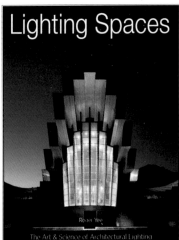
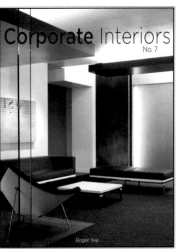

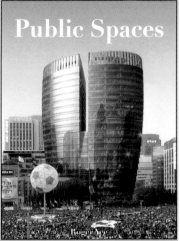
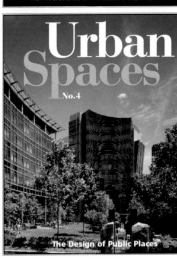
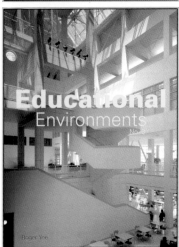

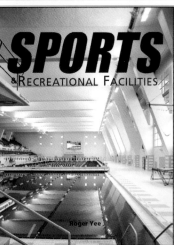

Advertiser Index